Cambridge Elements

Elements in the Gothic
edited by
Dale Townshend
Manchester Metropolitan University
Angela Wright
University of Sheffield

THE LAST MAN
AND GOTHIC SYMPATHY

Michael Cameron
Dalhousie University

CAMBRIDGE
UNIVERSITY PRESS

CAMBRIDGE
UNIVERSITY PRESS

Shaftesbury Road, Cambridge CB2 8EA, United Kingdom

One Liberty Plaza, 20th Floor, New York, NY 10006, USA

477 Williamstown Road, Port Melbourne, VIC 3207, Australia

314–321, 3rd Floor, Plot 3, Splendor Forum, Jasola District Centre,
New Delhi – 110025, India

103 Penang Road, #05–06/07, Visioncrest Commercial, Singapore 238467

Cambridge University Press is part of Cambridge University Press & Assessment,
a department of the University of Cambridge.

We share the University's mission to contribute to society through the pursuit of
education, learning and research at the highest international levels of excellence.

www.cambridge.org
Information on this title: www.cambridge.org/9781009494526

DOI: 10.1017/9781009357500

When citing this work, please include a reference to the DOI 10.1017/9781009357500

First published 2024

A catalogue record for this publication is available from the British Library.

ISBN 978-1-009-49452-6 Hardback
ISBN 978-1-009-35753-1 Paperback
ISSN 2634-8721 (online)
ISSN 2634-8713 (print)

The Last Man and Gothic Sympathy

Elements in the Gothic

DOI: 10.1017/9781009357500
First published online: February 2024

Michael Cameron
Dalhousie University

Author for correspondence: Michael Cameron, cameron.m@dal.ca

Abstract This *Element* explores the theme of 'Gothic sympathy' as it appears in a collection of 'Last Man' novels. A liminal site of both possibility and irreconcilability, Gothic sympathy at once challenges the anthropocentric bias of traditional notions of sympathetic concern, premising compassionate relations with other beings – animal, vegetal, and so on – beyond the standard measure of the liberal-humanist subject, and at the same time acknowledges the horror that is the ineluctable and untranslatable otherness accompanying, interrupting and shaping such a sympathetic connection. Many examples of 'Last Man' fiction explore the dialectical impasse of Gothic sympathy by dramatising complicated relationships between a lone liberal-humanist subject and (often monstrous) other-than-human or posthuman subjects that will persist beyond humanity's extinction. Such confrontations as they appear in Mary Shelley's *The Last Man*, H.G. Wells's *The Time Machine* and Richard Matheson's *I Am Legend* will be explored.

Keywords: Gothic, sympathy, last man, apocalypse, science fiction

ISBNs: 9781009494526 (HB), 9781009357531 (PB), 9781009357500 (OC)
ISSNs: 2634-8721 (online), 2634-8713 (print)

Contents

1 Gothic Sympathy and the Last Man

This *Element* explores the theme of 'Gothic sympathy' as it appears in a collection of 'Last Man' novels. Both terms require some explanation. I propose 'Gothic sympathy' as a concept without precise denotative demarcations but rather as a liminal site of both possibility and irreconcilability. It at once challenges the anthropocentric bias of traditional notions of sympathetic concern, premising compassionate relations with other beings – animal, vegetal, and so on – beyond the standard measure of the liberal-humanist subject, and at the same time acknowledges the horror that is the ineluctable and untranslatable otherness accompanying, interrupting and shaping such a sympathetic connection, for to preserve the Other's otherness in the sympathetic exchange, one must render oneself vulnerable to the Other, to their inexorable alien agency and to their potentially threatening influence. As for the 'Last Man',[1] I have in mind that subgenre of apocalyptic literature – itself a meeting place between the Gothic and science fiction – that imagines what it might be like to be the last human being on earth. Works that adhere to such a mode span disparate centuries and genres, from Cousin de Grainville's 1805 Miltonic prose poem *Le Dernier Homme* [*The Last Man*] to the 2015 comedy series *The Last Man on Earth* starring Will Forte and Kristen Shaal. Many examples of Last Man fiction explore the dialectical impasse of Gothic sympathy by dramatising complicated relationships between a lone liberal-humanist subject and (often monstrous) other-than-human or posthuman subjects that will persist beyond humanity's extinction. These works are thus fertile sites for the interrogation of Other-oriented emotional states, which is to say for the interrogation of sympathy and its vicissitudes.

The works analysed in this *Element* do not merely depict kinds or forms of sympathy that have been rendered Gothic; rather, they render bare the inherent Gothic nature of all sympathetic relations. Sympathy sports all the trappings of such a mode. In the truly sympathetic exchange, the bounds between Self and Other weaken, borders become porous, difference is traversed – is this not the very definition of the 'monstrous'? As Jeffrey Jerome Cohen states in his influential essay on the figure of the monster across cultures, '[i]n its function as dialectical Other or third-term supplement, the monster is an incorporation of

---

[1] Despite the rightfully antiquated use of 'man' and masculine pronouns to refer to a single specimen of the human species, I retain throughout the gendered nature, name and pronouns of the 'Last Man', for it is a trope that should be understood and interrogated as traditionally gendered. Though the reasons are far too many to explain here, the characters cast to embody this trope are almost ubiquitously gendered male not only on account of a Western-centric cultural bias that sees men as the normative standard, but also because the patriarchal Adam (as well as his derivatives, notably Noah) is a recurring allusion overlaid onto this character. To use the more general 'last person' would be to obfuscate a significant symbolic allusion that threads almost all of the representations of this figure.

the Outside, the Beyond – of all those loci that are rhetorically placed as distant and distinct but originate Within'.[2] I feel what you feel as you feel what I feel; I incorporate you as you incorporate I. Together we become a hybrid being through our sympathetic merger, an amalgamation, an emotional and existential monster. Consider the Gothic resonances of this famous and oft-cited passage from Adam Smith's *Theory of Moral Sentiments*:

> By the imagination we place ourselves in [another's] situation, we conceive ourselves enduring all the same torments, we enter as it were into his body, and become in some measure the same person with him, and thence form some idea of his sensations, and even feel something which, though weaker in degree, is not altogether unlike them. His agonies, when they are thus brought home to ourselves, when we have thus adopted and made them our own, begin at last to affect us, and we then tremble and shudder at the thought of what he feels.

Here, Smith describes sympathy in distinctly Gothic terms, as a kind of bodily possession or telepathic parasitism through which we gain access to another intimate emotional experience. Smith would double down on his use of Gothic imagery, describing the function of sympathetic resentment against a murderer as a kind of vengeful reanimation, a 're-animosity' perhaps:

> If the injured should perish in the quarrel, we not only sympathize with the real resentment of his friends and relations, but with the imaginary resentment which in fancy we lend to the dead, who is no longer capable of feeling that or any other human sentiment ... [W]e put ourselves in his situation, as we enter, as it were, into his body, and in our imaginations, in some measure, animate anew the deformed and mangled carcass of the slain.[3]

Sympathy has thus always been Gothic, is always-already Gothic, for the sympathetic Other that stands before my very Self is a Gothic double akin to the reflection in the mirror that moves on its own.[4]

This *Element* is situated within two related subfields of the Gothic: the ecoGothic and the posthuman Gothic. According to Sharae Deckard, '[i]f Gothic is characterised by excess, in Ecogothic [*sic*] environments are themselves excessive, sites of monstrous fecundity that threaten human civilisation, where vines and vegetation run rampant, or where plagues and vermin

[2] Jeffrey Jerome Cohen, 'Monster Culture (Seven Theses)', in Asa Simon Mittman and Marcus Hensel (eds.), *Classic Readings on Monster Theory* (Leeds: Arc Humanities Press, 2020), pp. 43–54 (pp. 46–47).

[3] Adam Smith, *The Theory of Moral Sentiments*, edited by Knud Haakonssen (Cambridge: Cambridge University Press, 2002), pp. 12, 82.

[4] For more on the Gothic double, Romanticism, and sympathy, see Benjamin Eric Daffron, *Romantic Doubles: Sex and Sympathy in British Gothic Literature 1790–1830* (New York: AMS Press, 2002).

spread deliriums'.[5] For the Last Man, this monstrous fecundity has for the most part won out and human 'civilisation' (however defined) is rendered a thing of the past. And yet, as Andrew Smith and William Hughes point out, while 'nature becomes constituted in the Gothic as a space of crisis', this crisis also 'conceptually creates a point of contact with the ecological'.[6] The Last Man cannot turn away from this point of contact, cannot quarantine the ecological beyond the bounds of the urban, and thus he must confront the ecological Other in ways that will test the ontological stability of his human Self. Already we are treading upon the territory of the posthuman Gothic. In the words of Anya Heise-von der Lippe, 'posthuman Gothic texts . . . highlight the instability and ultimate unsustainability of our most basic ontological category the human – along with the essential ethical and epistemological paradigms we derive from it'.[7] By feeling sympathy for and seeking sympathy with non-human Others, the Last Man necessarily engages in this ontologic destabilisation of the categorical human. As a result, the Last Man often experiences his own 'monstrification'[8] as his inability to mark stable demarcations become increasingly apparent. The 'human' subject thus becomes increasingly indistinguishable from that of the 'abhuman', which Kelly Hurley describes as 'a not-quite-human subject, characterized by its morphic variability, continually in danger of becoming not-itself, becoming other'. As it is for Hurley's 'abhuman', Gothic sympathy also 'resonat[es]' with Kristeva's 'abjection',[9] for it too 'simultaneously beseeches and pulverises the subject'. If it is true, as Kristeva states, that 'I experience abjection only if an Other has settled in place and stead of what will be "me"',[10] then Gothic sympathy is abjection wedded to its opposite: my Self has settled in place and stead of what should be an Other.

---

[5] Sharae Deckard, 'Ecogothic', in Maisha Webster and Xavier Aldana Reyes (eds.), *Twenty-First Century Gothic: An Edinburgh Companion* (Edinburgh: Edinburgh University Press, 2021), pp. 174–188 (p. 174).

[6] Andrew Smith and William Hughes, 'Introduction: Defining the ecoGothic', in Andrew Smith and William Hughes (eds.), *EcoGothic* (Manchester: Manchester University Press, 2013), pp. 1–14 (p. 3).

[7] Anya Heise-von der Lippe, 'Posthuman Gothic', in Maisha Webster and Xavier Aldana Reyes (eds.), *Twenty-First Century Gothic: An Edinburgh Companion* (Edinburgh: Edinburgh University Press, 2021), pp. 218–230 (p. 218). See also Anya Heise-von der Lippe 'Introduction: Post/human/Gothic', in Anya Heise-von der Lippe (ed.), *Posthuman Gothic* (Cardiff: University of Wales Press, 2017), pp. 1–16.

[8] Chris Koenig-Woodyard, 'The Mathematics of Monstrosity: Vampire Demography in Richard Matheson's *I Am Legend*', *University of Toronto Quarterly* 87:1 (Winter 2018): 81–109 (p. 85).

[9] Kelly Hurley, *The Gothic Body: Sexuality, Materialism, and Degeneration at the Fin de Siècle* (Cambridge: Cambridge University Press, 2004), pp. 3–4.

[10] Julia Kristeva, *Powers of Horror: An Essay on Abjection* (New York: Columbia University Press, 1982), pp. 5, 10.

Abjection, abhuman, posthuman Gothic, ecoGothic – all imbricate and interweave in the Last Man's experience of Gothic sympathy. For this study, I have chosen to focus on the 'Big Three', so to speak, of the Last Man genre: Mary Shelley's *The Last Man* (1826), H.G. Wells's *The Time Machine* (1895) and Richard Matheson's *I Am Legend* (1954). Each appearing during heightened periods of popularity regarding the trope of the Last Man, these texts remain the best known and most discussed works from their respective periods. Shelley's text appeared at the tail end of the Last Man's first major period of popularity in England, which began with a pirated English translation of Grainville's *Le Dernier Homme* in 1806 and saw the publication of many poems on the topic, including Byron's 'Darkness' (1816), Thomas Campbell's 'The Last Man' (1823) and Thomas Hood's 'The Last Man' (1826). Along with Camille Flammarion's *La Fin du Monde* (1893) and M.P. Shiel's *The Purple Cloud* (1901), Wells's novel reflected a renewed interest in the figure during the European fin de siècle. Matheson's novel joined Pat Frank's *Mr. Adam* (1946) and Mordecai Roshwald's *Level 7* (1959) in bringing the Last Man into the post-nuclear age. Though many of these other texts would have fit the theme, the three texts chosen for this study best exemplify the complex tensions and transformations of Gothic sympathy. Shelley's *The Last Man*, topic of Section 2, explores the irresolvable contradiction that is the desire for sympathy. Like a plague, sympathy is dangerous to the sanctity of the Self, yet the Last Man cannot live comfortably without it. Thus, Shelley reveals the monstrous hybridity of the living human being, a being neither at home in nature nor amongst the Platonic ideality of the 'abstract human'. Wells's *The Time Machine*, topic of Section 3, pits a time travelling Last Man against two evolutionary offshoots of humanity: the humanoid yet ineffectual Eloi and the bestial yet resourceful Morlocks. By sympathising only with the former and despising the latter, the Time Traveller demonstrates the vanity of sympathetic processes while at the same time modelling compassionate relations with livestock and animal test subjects; these sympathies are fickle, however, and can provide little more than a voyeuristic window into the suffering of an inherently violent and bloodthirsty natural world. Matheson's *I Am Legend*, topic of the final section, sees a lone Last Man barricade his house against a vampire horde. A dialectic of sympathy plays out as the Last Man engages in a succession of opportunities to foster sympathetic relations: first with a sickly dog, then with a woman who turns out to be a vampire, and then with a new society of 'living' (as opposed to 'undead') vampires. Ultimately, Matheson's Last Man will find himself at once sympathetically transformed into a new legendary monster in the eyes of this vampire society while at the same time capable of a posthuman sympathy with the undead vampires that are themselves hunted down by this society. In all three cases, sympathy complicates relations at the same time that it fosters them, as the Last Man struggles to understand himself and his place in a world that can only look back at him with unfamiliar eyes.

1.1 Sympathy's Slippery Definition

Like the boundaries of identity that it muddles and dissolves, sympathy boasts a highly rich and unstable list of potential definitions. Along with its adjectival, verbal and adverbial forms, 'sympathy' can be used to denote a wide field of emotional, psychic and social phenomena, all of which are conceptually distinguishable but are nonetheless so tightly interwoven in real experience that any attempt at categorical exactitude is bound for failure. Complicating matters further is sympathy's similarity to related terms such as compassion, pity and empathy. Empathy has to some extent supplanted these other concepts, including sympathy, as it has become a hot topic in neurology and psychology research within the last few decades.[11] This terminological shift in focus by no means implies, however, that there are clearly delineated or agreed-upon differences between these various terms in scientific or philosophical spheres, and the distinction between 'empathy' and 'sympathy' is at any rate meaningless when considering texts written before the twentieth century, as 'empathy' would be coined only in 1909.[12] My own instinct is to use 'compassion' to denote cases where one is acting upon an impulse to help someone in need; to use 'pity' in cases where one feels a distinct emotion towards another who is suffering; to use 'empathy' in cases where, when witnessing another's expression of their internal emotional state, one reactively and without conscious thought takes on an analogous emotional state; and to use 'sympathy' to denote this entire spectrum of Other-orientedness. While I will generally stick to these definitions over the course of this book, such definitions are by no means concrete, and I suspect it likely that were one to survey any random population on the relative differences between these concepts, one would end up with a widely varying set of definitions. Furthermore, one may, even with these tentative definitions, still feel the impulse to lock down a clear definition of just what one means by 'sympathy' and to support such a definition with strong justification. One would then be forced to choose between a formalist and

---

[11] See Jean Decety and William Ickes (eds.), *The Social Neuroscience of Empathy* (Cambridge, MA: MIT Press, 2009).

[12] 'Empathy' was coined by Edward Titchener as an English translation of the German term 'Einfühlung' in 1909, though the term would not adopt its current meaning until the 1940s. See Laura Hyatt Edward, 'A Brief Conceptual History of Einfühlung: 18th-Century Germany to Post-World War II U.S. Psychology', *History of Psychology* 16:4 (2013): 269–281.

a historicist approach: either define what sympathy is in itself and stick with that definition throughout, or apply to any individual text only those conceptions of sympathy that were understood during the era in which it appeared.[13]

Neither approach, however, is sufficient, at least for my project. If we seek a formalist definition, we are left asking – on whose authority should we take our definition? Philosophers who have tackled the nature of sympathy have not at all agreed on its workings and its nature. Consider, for instance, the differences in opinion between David Hume and Adam Smith, perhaps the two best known eighteenth-century philosophers of sympathy. For Hume, sympathy was akin to a physical reaction following mechanical laws like those of harmonic resonance:

> The minds of all men are similar in their feelings and operations, nor can any one be actuated by any affection, of which all others are not, in some degree, susceptible. As in strings equally wound up, the motion of one communicates itself to the rest; so all the affections readily pass from one person to another, and beget correspondent movements in every human creature.[14]

For Smith, conversely, sympathy was not quite so affectively immediate but required the help of the imagination to act as a mediator:

> As we have no immediate experience of what other men feel, we can form no idea of the manner in which they are afforded, but by conceiving what we ourselves should feel in the like situation. Though our brother is upon the rack, as long as we ourselves are at our ease, our senses will never inform us of what he suffers. They never did, and never can, carry us beyond our own person, and it is by the imagination only that we can form any conception of what are his sensations.[15]

The difference is a subtle but important one, for Hume leans more toward a passive form of empathic emotional contagion whereas Smith leaves more room for an active form of deliberate compassion.[16] To choose one over the other, then, would mean arbitrarily leaving aside a significant portion of sympathy's common connotations. Appeals to the reductionism of twentieth- and

---

[13] There is admittedly a third option – a prescriptivist approach would consider how we *should* or *ought* to define sympathy for any socially conscious or ethical reasons. Though it suggests some interesting questions, such an approach is not applicable for this *Element*.

[14] David Hume, *A Treatise of Human Nature*, pp. 575–576. https://davidhume.org/texts/t/full [last accessed 1 September 2023].

[15] Smith, *Moral Sentiments*, p. 11.

[16] For more on the differences between Hume and Smith, see Jeanne M. Britton, *Vicarious Narratives: A Literary History of Sympathy, 1750–1850* (Oxford: Oxford University Press, 2019), pp. 10–14 and Janis McLarren Caldwell, *Literature and Medicine in Nineteenth-Century Britain: From Mary Shelley to George Eliot* (Cambridge: Cambridge University Press, 2004), pp. 31–33.

twenty-first-century science for a clearly delineated definition are no more fruitful, for neurologists and psychologists are in no greater agreement over how best to define these terms, and any choice here would be just as arbitrary.[17] Regardless, any attempt to pin down a single working definition of 'sympathy' is not merely arbitrary but is also extremely limiting, for to reduce the rich complexity of sympathy to a single emotion or behaviour is only to impoverish one's study before one has even begun.

A major contributing factor behind this definitional complication is, of course, the fact that 'sympathy' has often found itself a contested term, and a historicist approach has the benefit of revealing the origins of these competing definitions and their transformations from one era to the next. Such is true for any term or concept, of course, as a word's etymology is by definition never static but is twisted and contorted by the pressures and requirements of historical context. This etymological transformation is especially true of 'sympathy', however, as the word has been subject to a great deal of philosophical, political and scientific scrutiny from at least the seventeenth through to the twenty-first centuries. As is well known, the long eighteenth century was a fertile period for philosophies of sympathy, and given it directly preceded and arguably influenced and informed the centuries that followed, it is worth giving a very brief account of sympathy's development during this period.

Stemming from the use of the term *sympatheia* in ancient Stoic thought, sympathy had originally referred to harmony amongst any and all things in nature – including human beings – and such a notion of sympathy was often imbued with occult or magical connotations.[18] Approaching the eighteenth century, however, things changed. As a result of the enlightenment, 'nature and mind were torn apart', and thus 'sympathy could now play a role only within the affective sphere of the mind'.[19] Sympathy, then, would have to be redefined to adapt to new scientific and philosophical views regarding the nature of reality. At the same time, Europe generally and England particularly during this period saw the budding economic and political individualism that would blossom into nineteenth-century Liberalism, and many turned to sympathy as the intersubjective solution for reaffirming national and social unity.[20] The long

---

[17] See C. Daniel Batson, 'These Things Called Empathy: Eight Related but Distinct Phenomena', in Jean Decety and William Ickes (eds.), *The Social Neuroscience of Empathy* (Cambridge: MIT Press, 2009), pp. 3–15.

[18] See Roman Alexander Barton, Alexander Klaudies and Thomas Micklich, 'Introduction', in Roman Alexander Barton, Alexander Klaudies and Thomas Micklich (eds.), *Sympathy in Transformation: Dynamics Between Rhetorics, Poetics and Ethics* (Berlin, Boston: De Gruyter, 2018), pp. 1–16 (p. 2) and Caldwell, *Literature and Medicine*, p. 30.

[19] Roman Alexander Barton, Alexander Klaudies and Thomas Micklich, 'Introduction', pp. 6–7.

[20] See Daffron, *Romantic Doubles,* pp. 6–10.

eighteenth century, then, was primed for a lengthy debate about both the nature and relative merits of sympathy, a debate in which Hume and Smith both participated. Jonathan Lamb identifies five different types of sympathy that arose during this period: 'mechanical', that is, sympathy as a physical effect of the nervous system; 'sociable', that is, sympathy as the social impulse to help others; 'theatrical', that is, sympathy as the (real or imagined) witnessing of another's suffering; 'complete', that is, sympathy as the (albeit illusory) experience of fully adopting the identity and experience of another; and 'horrid', that is, any 'sympathy that … seemed to go too far' in transgressing categorical difference.[21] As is well known, this same period also saw the rise of the novel, which throughout the eighteenth and well into the nineteenth centuries inspired both support and condemnation for its purported ability to incite the sympathies of its readers.[22] Not only did thoughts about sympathy shape how people thought about novels, but novels themselves shaped how people thought about sympathy. According to Jeanne M. Britton, whereas philosophers like Hume and Smith tended to consider sympathy primarily in terms of similitude, novelists between 1750 and 1850 'redefine[d] sympathy as a novelistic phenomenon by staging scenes of sympathy between characters whose affinities suggest figurative kinships but whose differences stretch the limits of resemblance'.[23] By the nineteenth century, then, sympathy had taken on a whole host of connotations, and it would only continue to do so as time went on.

Given the rich, yet far from exhaustive, list of shifting connotations given in this sketch, it would seem that the historicist approach might in fact be the most beneficial. Admittedly, I am more inclined towards defending such a position over that of the formalist or scientifically reductionist, for I agree with Rob Boddice that 'emotions have a history' and that there is value to be had in 'disrupt[ing] and defamiliari[sing] concepts, emotions, and moral categories that we perhaps take for granted'.[24] And yet, the historicist approach is itself not completely satisfying, at least for this *Element*, for two significant reasons. First, given the wide historical scope of this *Element*, it is important that we remain able to compare texts across distant chronological gaps. If *The Last Man* of 1826 and *I Am Legend* of 1954 depict or describe a similar phenomenon, we want to be able to speak of both depictions even if the former calls it 'sympathy'

---

[21] See Jonathan Lamb, *The Evolution of Sympathy in the Long Eighteenth Century* (London: Pickering & Chatto, 2009), pp. 41–76, 105–128.

[22] See Section 2.2 of this *Element* and Suzanne Keen, *Empathy and the Novel* (New York: Oxford University Press, 2007), pp. 37–39, 44–55.

[23] Britton, *Vicarious Narrative*, 5

[24] Rob Boddice, *The Science of Sympathy: Morality, Evolution, and Victorian Civilization* (Illinois: University of Illinois, 2016), pp. 5, 6.

and the latter calls it 'empathy'. Second, and perhaps more importantly, the various types and definitions of sympathy recounted above by no means succeed and replace each other but rather accrue such that sympathy can at any moment connote any combination of these meanings. To use a musical metaphor of which Hume would most likely approve, it is as if 'sympathy' is itself a string tightly strung, and each new connotation added to the term is but a higher overtone such that the vibration of the single word evokes a rich and complex harmony. To put it another way, sympathy is messy. But perhaps it should remain that way. The sympathetic exchange is itself messy: identities merge; boundaries between 'I' and 'You', 'Self' and 'Other' are rendered porous and traversable; attempts to uphold categorical demarcations are rendered futile. I suggest it is the same with our emotional states. Trying to untangle the Gordian knot of emotions either to categorise or to historicise sympathy and its various derivatives can be a useful exercise up to a point, as long as we do so in full acceptance of the fact that such ventures are always provisional and prone to slippage.

1.2 (Gothic) Sympathy in *Frankenstein*

For an example both of sympathy's plurality and of its Gothic side, let us consider an archetypal case: Mary Shelley's *Frankenstein*. Sympathy is a central preoccupation of *Frankenstein*'s narrative, and scholars have explored the ways in which the novel depicts at once the longing for sympathetic connection, the failures of sympathetic appeals and the dangers of sympathetic excess. However, that sympathy is central to *Frankenstein* by no means suggests that the novel has a singular or clearly delineated notion of the concept. Far from it, in fact. Notably, the complex and irreducible senses given to the term persist across the various editions of the text. As is well known, Shelley made several revisions (some minor, some significant) to the novel between the original 1818 publication and the 1831 edition, the most notable being the greater emphasis placed on the domestic sphere and the 'quasi-religious faith' that the 1831 edition 'vests in the love of friends and family'.[25] Yet, even with such changes, sympathy remains multivalent, irreconcilable and indeed Gothic throughout the various editions, as demonstrated by the following examples which notably remain unchanged between editions.[26]

---

[25] Jennifer L. Airey, *Religion Around Mary Shelley* (University Park: Pennsylvania University Press, 2019), p. 136.

[26] To avoid weighing in on the respective editorial authority of either version, I rely on the Broadview edition which includes the entirety of the 1818 edition and a thorough appendix of Shelley's later changes. In addition to each passage quoted herein remaining unchanged between

Sympathy's conceptual plurality is evident immediately in the novel's epistolary frame narrative. Walton, writing to his sister while travelling companionless to the North Pole, uses sympathy to denote many related, yet nonetheless different, emotional and psychic phenomena. That Shelley at times uses sympathy to denote something closer to 'empathy' – that is, sympathy as a mostly passive experience of taking on another's emotional state – is evident when Walton describes his own experience of witnessing Victor Frankenstein's suffering: 'his constant and deep grief fills me with sympathy and compassion . . . He excites at once my admiration and my pity . . . How can I see so noble a creature destroyed by misery without feeling the most poignant grief?' Here, Walton juxtaposes sympathy against compassion, as if to differentiate the passive and proto-empathic experience of feeling another's grief to the active desire to show compassion to another. Yet, Walton's interactions with Victor also bestow upon sympathy an active capacity, for when Walton expresses his 'desire to ameliorate [Victor's] fate', Victor responds by thanking Walton 'for [his] sympathy'. Here, sympathy is not merely an empathic reflex but is understood as an intentional act of compassion, a step from passive to active emotion. Completing this Hegelian-esque dialectic, Walton suggests a synthesis of the passive empathetic sympathy and the active compassionate sympathy in the sympathy of mutual understanding when, before meeting Victor, he expresses to his sister that he 'desire[s] the company of a man who could sympathize with me; whose eyes would reply to mine'.[27] The sympathy Walton seeks here is not merely the vicarious experience of the emotional state *of* another or a feeling of compassion *for* another; rather, he seeks a deeper sense of companionship and understanding *with* one who can appreciate his feelings and recognise the existence of his own emotional, inner world.

The creature's story at the novel's centre is itself rife with invocations of sympathy, and here too we find the word used in a multiplicity of senses. In addition to uses like those aforementioned, the creature also uses sympathy to denote something like romantic love or domestic partnership, asking Victor to 'create a female for me, with whom I can live in the interchange of those sympathies necessary for my being'. Victor later reinforces this interpretation of the term, relating sympathy with sexual desire. Contemplating the ethics of building a female for the creature, Victor worries that he might help bring about a 'race of devils', for 'one of the first results of those sympathies for which the daemon thirsted would be children'. Notable too is the fact that the creature uses

editions, any alterations to the context in which these passages originally appear is marginal and ultimately insignificant for the meaning of the included passages.

27 Mary Shelley, *Frankenstein; or, the Modern Prometheus*, edited by D. L. Macdonald and Kathleen Scherf (Peterborough: Broadview, 2012), pp. 60–61, 62, 54.

sympathy to denote the sharing not only of the negative but also of the positive emotions of others, as is evident in the creature's account of his time spying on the lives of the De Lacy family: 'The gentle manners of the cottagers greatly endeared them to me: when they were unhappy, I felt depressed; when they rejoiced, I sympathized in their joys'.[28] The nature of sympathy, in brief, is thus for Shelley as irreducibly multiple as the body of Frankenstein's composite creation.

Likely as a result of such a multivalent depiction of sympathy in the text, scholarly responses to the topic have been varied. David Marshall's early work on the topic, *The Surprising Effects of Sympathy: Marivaux, Diderot, Rousseau, and Mary Shelley*, identifies 'an ambivalent view of sympathy' in Shelley's first novel, one that encompasses 'the dangerous effects of both sympathy and a lack of sympathy: the failure to recognize others as fellow creatures with fellow feeling turns both oneself and others into monsters, while sympathy itself seems to result in monstrous forms of reproduction'. Despite this recognition of sympathy's inherent ambiguity in the text, Marshall ultimately prioritises the lack of sympathy as taken up in the novel, noting that his chapter on Shelley 'specifically focuses on the causes and effects of sympathy's failure'.[29] For some time, scholars followed Marshall's lead. For example, Janis McLarren Caldwell argues that though '[t]he plot of *Frankenstein* ... repeatedly dramatizes the failure of social sympathy', such depictions are potentially a 'heuristic device' for the sake of fostering a more ethical kind of sympathetic relation. Thus, argues Caldwell, Shelley 'succeeds ... in elaborating a different kind of sympathy, one that suspends judgment and labors for the understanding of otherness'.[30] In these and other earlier interpretations,[31] failure to foster sympathetic connection results in spite of, rather than because of, sympathy and its supposed virtues; much more recently, however, scholars have returned to the notion that sympathy itself might be dangerous in *Frankenstein* 'even when it is in rich supply'.[32] This scholarly re-evaluation pertains most to sympathy for the creature, who for Erin M. Goss is 'an embodiment of the most banal and everyday form of misogyny'. 'What is striking', Goss elaborates, 'is that sympathy for the creature, so often understood as allegorical

---

[28] Shelley, *Frankenstein*, pp. 156, 174, 129.

[29] David Marshall, *The Surprising Effects of Sympathy: Marivaux, Diderot, Rousseau, and Mary Shelley* (Chicago: The University of Chicago Press, 1988), pp. 213, 181.

[30] Caldwell, *Literature and Medicine*, pp. 42, 37.

[31] Other examples include the respective chapters on *Frankenstein* in both Daffron's *Romantic Doubles* and Britton's *Vicarious Narratives*.

[32] Michelle Faubert, 'Challenging Sympathy in Mary Shelley's Fiction: *Frankenstein, Matilda*, and "The Mourner"', *English: Journal of the English Association* 71:275 (2022): 315–332 (p. 319).

sympathy for various marginalized and other groups, risks crystallizing into
the sympathy demanded by the man who can't get a date and therefore decides
to destroy the world that he is convinced owes him one'.[33] Michelle Faubert
echoes this concern, observing astutely that '[t]oday, we might even go so far
as to call the monster an "incel" murderer, an involuntary celibate who
believes his lack of a romantic partner constitutes his right to kill others in
protest'.[34] And yet, as both Goss and Faubert note, readers tend overwhelm-
ingly to sympathise with the creature. I can attest to such a claim – teaching the
novel, I have observed that the instinct of many students is to sympathise,
often uncritically, with the creature.

Building here on Goss and Faubert, we might say that the sympathetic
reader falls prey to the creature's eloquent speech because they do not follow
Walton's lead as demonstrated during the explorer's sole confrontation with
Victor's creation. After discovering that the being has boarded the ship to pay
respects to his deceased creator, Walton engages in conversation with the
creature and at first feels a 'mixture of curiosity and compassion'. Notably,
Walton avoids looking upon the face of the creature during their conversation,
and thus like the reader, Walton is both free from the prejudice-inspiring
image of the monster's profound ugliness and free to sympathise with the
creature's story of abandonment and suffering. And yet, Walton ultimately
rejects any sympathy he might have initially felt: 'I was at first touched by the
expressions of his misery; yet when I called to mind what Frankenstein had
said of his powers of eloquence and persuasion, and when I again cast my eyes
on the lifeless form of my friend, indignation was rekindled within me'.[35]
Walton is sceptical towards the creature's methods of persuasive speech,
suspecting him of using sympathetic language as a form of emotional manipulation. In his own contribution to this *Elements* series, Matt Foley notes that
the creature's monstrous image is not mirrored in the tone or timbre of the
creature's voice:

> It is the creature's visage and, eventually, its murderous actions, that set the
> parameters of its monstrosity. Its voice, however, is lofty and articulate, even
> human. Monstrous voices, I suggest, emerge fully in the soundworld of the
> Gothic of the decades that follow the publication of Shelley's revised edition
> of *Frankenstein* in 1831.[36]

[33] Erin M. Goss, 'The Smiles that One Is Owed: Justice, Justine, and Sympathy for a Wretch', in
Orrin N. C. Wang (ed.), *Frankenstein in Theory* (New York: Bloomsbury Academic, 2021), pp.
185–198 (p. 187).
[34] Faubert, 'Challenging Sympathy', p. 321.   [35] Shelley, *Frankenstein*, pp. 217, 218.
[36] Matt Foley, *Gothic Voices: The Vococentric Soundworld of Gothic Writing* (Cambridge:
Cambridge University Press, 2023), p. 25.

Foley's claim is certainly true of the tonal and rhetorical quality of the creature's voice and diction, but is there not something monstrous about an eloquent speech that seeks to persuade another that their envy-induced homicides are justified? Walton's reaction to the creature's appeal for sympathy suggests that such a voice is indeed monstrous. Walton, like the sympathetic reader, does not judge based on the creature's frightening image; unlike the sympathetic reader, the explorer feels contempt nonetheless, a contempt that is more than merely 'skin-deep'.

Taken together, these observations give a comprehensive picture of Gothic sympathy. In *Frankenstein*, we find an unstable definition for 'sympathy', such that the borders between instinct and will, between passive and active, between empathy and compassion, and ultimately between Self and Other are blurred; we find a rejection of the monster that is itself a rejection of the monstrous Other in the Self, a form of sympathy that is indistinguishable from abjection; and we find a creeping suspicion that one's sympathies are merely the playthings for a manipulative voice and a scheming mind. Should they reflect on the full weight of this Gothic indeterminacy, the reader is left in a state of profound uncertainty regarding the creature. The character at once does and does not deserve our sympathy, is and is not guilty of his crimes, is and is not a manifestation of our own guilt and desire for absolution. The same might also be said for many of the characters in Shelley's *The Last Man*, to which we now turn.

2 Shelley's Infectious Despair

For a novel with such a title, *The Last Man* stars a surprisingly large cast of characters. Less a story about the Last Man and his solitary exploits than it is the character's origin story, Shelley's novel follows the life of Lionel Verney, the principal narrator of the novel destined by its end to become the eponymous character. The cause of humanity's almost complete eradication – a global plague pandemic – receives its first mention only in chapter twelve of thirty, and its rampage across the planet does not truly begin until the novel's halfway point. It is not until the final few chapters that Verney finds himself alone, having lost his family, his friends and all his acquaintances save a loyal dog. Nonetheless, as with the other novels considered in this study, much of Shelley's *The Last Man* is about tense and complicated sympathies between oneself and others, between Self and Other. The novel's characters seek sympathy and intimate connection with others, but this intimacy often leaves these characters vulnerable to harm. Even before the arrival of the plague, the emotional vicissitudes of interpersonal relationships lead to physical illness, suicide and untimely death; with the plague's arrival, sympathetic intimacy at once becomes dearer and more dangerous. Sympathy takes many forms in the novel, three of which interest us here: the first is sympathy of mutual understanding, which is at its most extreme that rare and intimate sympathy between two individuals, often lovers, who become as 'one heart, one hope, one life';[37] the second is sympathy as society-wide emotional and ideational contagion, what Burke called the 'contagion of the passions';[38] and the third is the cross-species sympathy between human beings and domestic animals. Each of these three forms, as we shall see over the course of this section, is rife with conceptual, emotional and moral complications, such that sympathy becomes, as Snyder says of the novel's depiction of plague, 'an irreducible phenomenon that both challenges and defines the limits of rational understanding'.[39]

This multivalent depiction of sympathy has led to a wide variety of scholarly interpretations of the theme, and as it was with *Frankenstein*, the status of sympathy in Shelley's *The Last Man* has gone through an academic re-evaluation in recent years, shifting from readings that interpret sympathy as either beneficial in its presence or detrimental only in its absence to those that read it as morally complicated at best and emotionally destructive at worst. An early champion of reading sympathy in *The Last Man* as possessing a transformative political potential is Jennifer A. Wagner-Lawler, who argues that the strength of Shelley's text lies 'in a feminizing insistence on sentiment, sympathy, and sociality designed to short-circuit a masculine narrative of the sublime'.[40] In a similar vein, Lauren Cameron argues that, in contradistinction to the Malthusianism of the day, Shelley instead foregrounds the 'ethical imperative of considering human suffering from an empathic position and on an individual level'.[41] Much more recently, however, scholars have taken a different approach to the topic. Shoshannah Bryn Jones Square distinguishes two different kinds of sympathy in *The Last Man*: 'therapeutic sympathy' and 'pathologic sympathy'. About the latter, which she identifies as characterising Perdita's destructive relationship with Lord Raymond in the novel, Bryn Jones Square states, 'when felt too excessively, sympathy can become pathological, its positive potential negated, and it may instead inflame the passions and

---

[37] Mary Shelley, *The Last Man*, edited by Anne McWhir (Peterborough: Broadview, 1996), p. 97.

[38] Edmund Burke, *A Philosophical Enquiry Into the Origin of Our Ideas of the Sublime and Beautiful*, edited by Adam Phillips (Oxford: Oxford University Press, 1998), p. 160.

[39] Robert Lance Snyder, 'Apocalypse and Indeterminacy in Mary Shelley's "The Last Man"', *Studies in Romanticism* 17:4 (Fall 1978): 435–452 (p. 437).

[40] Jennifer A. Wagner-Lawlor, 'Performing History, Performing Humanity in Mary Shelley's *The Last Man*', *SEL: Studies in English Literature 1500–1900* 42:4 (Autumn 2002): 753–780 (p. 771).

[41] Lauren Cameron, 'Mary Shelley's Malthusian Objections in *The Last Man*', *Nineteenth-Century Literature* 67:2 (September 2012): 177–203 (p. 196).

precipitate madness, alienation, and suicide'.[42] Similarly, Jennifer Deren characterises *The Last Man*'s blend of compassion and revulsion as 'a phenomenon [she] call[s] *revolting sympathies*'. Against those who read a failure of sympathy in Lionel's hostile encounter with the only explicitly Black character in the text, Deren states that 'the encounter has as much to do with the revolting operations of sympathy as with racial difference per se':

> Lionel 'enters' into the black man's suffering, feeling his ailments in and on his own body, in an experience that both we and the novel understand as sympathy. Contrary to expectations of compassion and benevolence, identification produces a kind of racism, a revolting response of 'horror and impatience' that arises out of and as part of sympathy's erasure of difference.

Though she does not invoke the Gothic in her description, Deren anticipates my own notion of Gothic sympathy when she notes that the episode's 'erasure of difference – represented as painful, terrifying, and repulsive – emerges as a constitutive possibility existing within the sympathetic encounter'.[43] Alongside the likes of Faubert and Goss as discussed in the previous section, Bryn Jones Square and Deren represent a sea change in the reading of sympathy in Shelley's work, no longer seeing it as simply beneficial or impotent but as messy, manipulative and threatening – and, we might add, Gothic.

As it is with the novel's depiction of sympathy, the form of *The Last Man* is akin to Shelley's most famous monstrous creation, for it is a Frankensteinian conjoining of parts that, at least at first glance, don't quite fit together. The major events of the first half take the most obvious form of a tragic novel of sensibility, rife with political intrigue and a doomed love triangle that ends in the (partially literal, partially figurative) suicides of all three involved; the major events of the second are more akin to a work of post-apocalyptic sci-fi, earning for the novel the moniker of 'the first major example of secular eschatology in literature'.[44] The novel's central event, around which the first and second halves of the novel gravitate as around an abysmal black hole, is the conquest of the plague-ridden Constantinople by an army of Greek liberationists. How should we read this apparent disjunction at the very centre of the text? In this section I argue that Shelley literalises the psychic process of despairing sympathies by dramatising the sympathetic 'entering into' of the (interpersonal) Other as the

---

[42] Shoshannah Bryn Jones Square, 'The "victim of too much loving": Perdita Verney's Self-Destructive Sympathy in Mary Shelley's *The Last Man*', *Studies in Literary Imagination* 51:1 (Spring 2018): 61–78 (pp. 64, 61).

[43] Jennifer Deren, 'Revolting Sympathies in Mary Shelley's The Last Man', *Nineteenth Century Literature* 72:2 (2017): 135–160 (pp. 138, 146, 144).

[44] W. Warren Wagar, *Terminal Visions: The Literature of Last Things* (Bloomington: Indiana University Press 1982), p. 13.

literal 'entering into' of the (orientalised) Other: the harmful and ultimately fatal process of Perdita's intimate sympathies with Lord Raymond is re-enacted in the conquest of Constantinople. Furthermore, we should read the resolution of the sentimental tragedy of the novel's first half as unleashing an 'effluvial despair' that is the very plague of the second half; just as there were fears that sentimental literature like Goethe's *The Sorrows of Young Werther* might unleash a suicidal contagion across Europe, so too does the fatal tragedy of Perdita and Raymond unleash a contagion of suicidal despair. An analysis of the world of unsympathetic indifference in which Verney ultimately finds himself will close the section; the ways in which such a solitary and unsympathetic state in essence 'monstrifies' Verney will look ahead to the remaining sections.

2.1 'Man a Microcosm of Nature'

The Last Man's first half is preoccupied with the intrigue of doomed love, particularly that between the ambitious yet impulsive Lord Raymond and Verney's reserved yet deep-feeling sister, Perdita. Raymond enters the narrative as a decorated war hero with bullish political aspirations, conspiring to restore the monarchy of the presently Republican England and to install himself on the throne by marrying Idris, the daughter of the former King and Queen. Immediately upon his arrival, Raymond sparks an emotional firestorm: Idris' brother Adrian – rightful claimant of the throne were he not a staunch support of Republican government – falls into a love-sick bout of illness when his beloved, the Greek princess Evadne, falls for Raymond and spurns Adrian's devotion. Yet, forgoing both the obsessive love of Evadne and the transactional prospects of Idris, Raymond follows the passions of his 'over-ruling heart' and chooses 'the rapture of assured sympathy' with Perdita, thus abandoning for the moment his political and military ambitions. Verney then marries Idris, and Adrian recovers from his despair-induced illness; for a time, these characters form a 'happy circle'[45] that has been widely acknowledged to reflect moments and members of Shelley's own life and family.[46]

Predictably, the happy times do not last. Lord Raymond, now Lord Protector of the Republican England, reunites with an impoverished Evadne, and what begins as a compassionate attempt to help an old friend becomes a secretive affair, such that Raymond is said to have 'bidden an eternal farewell to open-hearted converse, and entire sympathy with [Perdita,] the companion of his

---

[45] Shelley, *The Last Man*, pp. 50, 53, 70.

[46] See Anne McWhir, 'Introduction', in Mary Shelley, *The Last Man*, edited by Anne McWhir (Peterborough: Broadview, 1996), xiii–xxxvi (pp. xx–xxi), and Morton D. Paley, '*The Last Man*: Apocalypse Without Millennium', in Anne K. Mellor (ed.), *The Other Mary Shelley: Beyond Frankenstein* (Oxford: Oxford University Press, 1993), pp. 107–123 (pp. 109–110).

life'.[47] After his affair is revealed, Raymond renounces the protectorate and heads East to lead the Greeks in their war for independence against Turkish occupation. Perdita and Raymond reconcile in Greece before Raymond leads the army to the gates of Constantinople, setting up the tragic conclusion of this doomed romance plot. Evadne, disguised as a man so as to fight in the war, is discovered wounded and cursing Raymond with her dying breath; fully believing in the inevitability of the curse and wholeheartedly accepting its consequences, Raymond enters alone the plague-ridden Constantinople and dies in a explosion; grief-stricken and taken from Greece against her will by her brother, Perdita throws herself off a boat and drowns. It is only here, with the apparent resolution of this sentimental tragedy, that the plague can enter as the central driver of the remainder of the plot.

Raymond and Perdita's relationship is not only one of romantic love but also of intense sympathy, in the sense of a profound intimacy and deep understanding such that the pair becomes 'one heart, one hope, one life'.[48] For Shoshannah Bryn Jones Square, this sympathetic merger of identities is the ultimate cause of Perdita's doom: 'Exhibiting her sympathy to an "extreme" and "psychologically unhealthy" degree, Perdita loses her self [*sic*] in her pathological love for her husband Lord Raymond, a metaphorical annihilation of self that eventually leads to a literal annihilation of self'. In other words, Perdita merges her own identity so thoroughly to that of Raymond that she enacts 'a morbid forgetfulness of self'.[49] Bryn Jones Square's analysis is astute, and it is no failing on her part that she considers Raymond and Perdita's doomed love story as if the entire plague tale of the second half did not exist; the sentimental tragedy of the first half seems so wholly divorced from the second that the former can easily be analysed as if it were its own separate novel. Nonetheless, the suicidal sympathy of Raymond and Perdita is deeply connected with the latter plague pandemic on a metaphorical level, the two halves of the novel bound together by the conquest of the plague-ridden Constantinople. Simply put, Raymond's literal entering into the stronghold of the (orientalised) Other dramatises the sympathetic process of entering into the emotions of the (interpersonal) Other, and just as Perdita's intense sympathy with Raymond leaves her vulnerable to her partner's intense and fickle passions, so too does the entering of the British commander into Constantinople leave England itself vulnerable to the plague.

That the siege of the plague-ridden Constantinople mirrors England's own experience with the plague is made explicit in Verney's description of the latter: after the plague has reached England, Verney notes that 'the sea, late our

---

[47] Shelley, *The Last Man*, p. 94.   [48] Shelley, *The Last Man*, p. 97.
[49] Bryn Jones Square, 'Self-Destructive Sympathy', pp. 62, 69.

defence, seems our prison bound; hemmed in by its gulphs, we shall die like the famished inhabitants of a besieged town'.[50] This mirroring in effect literalises the sympathetic process, for just as an intense sympathy with another's inner experience is thought to transform oneself, as it were, into the other, so too does the 'entering into' of Constantinople eventually lead to Constantinople's 'entering into' England via the plague, transforming the latter country into a mirror image of the former.[51] Sympathy, after all, is often spoken about in terms of spatial and bodily metaphors. We speak of someone 'entering into' the mind and emotions of another; we speak of 'walking a mile in someone else's shoes'. Again, we are reminded of the metaphors from Smith's oft-cited passage: by way of the sympathetic imagination, 'we place ourselves in [another's] position' and 'enter as it were into [another's] body' that their sufferings 'might be brought home to ourselves'.[52] Michelle Faubert points out, however, that while 'Smith presents the process of sympathy as an externalization of the Self' into the Other, it is ultimately '[t]hrough the observer's imagination [that] the Other's feelings and experiences enter the Self and change it from within'.[53] This dialectic is enacted in the conquest of the plague-infested Constantinople. Raymond enters fearing he has already 'imbibed its effluvia', and thus his entering of Constantinople is at the same time the plague's entering of his lungs – the entering into the metonymic Other is in fact the entering of the Other into the Self. Lord Raymond even provides something of a philosophical justification for this metaphorical reading, musing at one point early in the text that '[p]hilosophers have called man a microcosm of nature, and find a reflection in the internal mind for all this machinery visible at work around us'.[54] The conquest of Constantinople represents the obverse counterpart to such a notion, a material macrocosm reflecting the workings of the internal mind and its sympathies.

In addition to these more abstract connections, Shelley also provides a rich trove of symbolism to rhetorically connect Raymond and Perdita's

---

[50] Shelley, *The Last Man*, p. 196.

[51] Such an idea reflects contemporary anxieties that British colonial ventures might bring back foreign disease or, worse, foreign ideas. For more, see Lee Sterrenburg, '*The Last Man*: Anatomy of a Failed Revolution', *Nineteenth-Century Fiction* 33:3 (December 1978): 324–347; Paul A. Cantor, 'The Apocalypse of Empire: Mary Shelley's *The Last Man*', in Sydney M. Conger, Frederick S. Frank, Gregory O'Dea (eds.), *Iconoclastic Departures: Mary Shelley After Frankenstein: Essays in Honor of the Bicentenary of Mary Shelley's Birth* (Madison: Fairleigh Dickinson University Press, 1997) pp. 193–211; and Anne McWhir, 'Mary Shelley's Anti-Contagionism: *The Last Man* as "Fatal Narrative"', *Mosaic: An Interdisciplinary Critical Journal* 35:2 (June 2002): 23–38.

[52] Smith, *Moral Sentiments*, p. 12.

[53] Michelle Faubert, '*Werther* Goes Viral: Suicidal Contagion, Anti-Vaccination, and Infectious Sympathy', *Literature and Medicine* 34:2 (Fall 2016): 389–417 (p. 398).

[54] Shelley, *The Last Man*, p. 147, 51.

intimate sympathy with the conquest of Constantinople. That Perdita and Constantinople are metaphorically linked is evident in their shared associated colour, for Perdita is described early in the novel as having 'golden hair' whereas Constantinople is repeatedly called the 'Golden City'. Further linking the woman with the city, the language Raymond uses to profess his love for Perdita and to enter into her sympathies mirrors the later events at Constantinople. To Perdita, Raymond likens his debate in Parliament the day previous to a 'wordy war' and explains his inspiration for engaging in it as 'a wish to appear before [Perdita], not vanquished, but as a conqueror'. He expresses a similar desire during the later war in the East, wishing to blaze a trail of victory that he might appear a conqueror before the larger city; '[b]efore the battle of Rodosto', explains Raymond, 'I was full of hope and spirit; to conquer there, and afterwards to take Constantinople, was the hope, the bourne, the fulfilment of my ambition'. To Perdita, Raymond describes the entering of her sympathies in spatial terms, asking that her 'entire heart ... open wide its door to admit [him] to its very centre'. Similar language is used to recount the later events: though the walls into Constantinople remain closed at first, Raymond eventually enters without resistance through a demolished gate into 'the heart of the city'. To Perdita, Raymond passionately declares '[t]ake me – mould me to your will, possess my heart and soul to all eternity'; in killing him within its walls, Constantinople is more truly the one to possess his soul 'to all eternity'. Admittedly, Raymond's conquest of Perdita's heart and his conquest of Constantinople seem to differ greatly in the willingness of the one being 'conquered', for unlike the garrison in Constantinople, Perdita assures Raymond that she 'needs no persuasion' to open up to him. However, by the time he enters Constantinople, Raymond has proven himself not above the use of emotional manipulation to get his way with Perdita, and thus we might read the earlier courtship as no less coercive than his latter conquests. The fate of Constantinople thus becomes the truest portrait of what follows from accepting Raymond's sympathies – 'wasted and haggard' inhabitants 'obliged to take refuge in their only hope – submission'.[55]

Yet, as is to be expected of characters who have so thoroughly sympathised to the point of merging their identities, the entering of Constantinople is similarly coded in terms of Perdita's 'entering into' a renewed sympathy with Raymond after his infidelity with Evadne. After noting that they had 'built a wall between them and the world', Verney describes the affair between Raymond and Evadne in siege-like terms: 'Without, a thousand harpies raved,

---

[55] Shelley, *The Last Man*, pp. 11, 143, 52, 144, 53, 156, 53, 146.

remorse and misery, expecting the destined moment for their invasion.[56] Verney *qua* narrator then links Constantinople with Raymond's secrecy by dressing the latter in orientalised imagery, noting that for Raymond, '[t]he veil must be thicker than that invented by Turkish jealousy; the wall higher than the unscalable tower of Vathek'.[57] Keeping the secret from Perdita, however, eats away at Raymond from the inside like the plague, for 'his spirit was as a pure fire, which fades and shrinks from every contagion of foul atmosphere: but now the contagion had become incorporated with its essence, and the change was the more painful'. The parallels between Raymond and Constantinople, then, are clear – just as the air inside Constantinople is plagued, so too is the secret inner life that Raymond has carved off from the one with whom he has pledged his love. For Perdita to enter again into an intimate, sympathetic relationship with Raymond would be to expose herself to this contagion, for 'she, even as a mirror, changed as he changed'.[58] Such exposure proves fatal: at the whims of his despairing passion, Raymond follows a suicidal drive into the heart of the plagued city; at the whims of her overwhelming grief, Perdita follows her own suicidal drive into the Mediterranean.

2.2 'The Feeling Was Infectious'

With the conquest of Constantinople comes the end of both Raymond and Perdita; far from over, however, are the effects of their despairing sympathies, which take the form of the plague that dominates the second half of the novel. The conquest of Constantinople is at least figuratively, and perhaps literally, the cause of the plague's transition from a localised epidemic to a global pandemic. This causal connection is dramatised in Lionel Verney's oft-cited nightmare amongst the ruins of Constantinople. After collapsing of exhaustion while searching for Raymond, Verney dreams up an image of Raymond as a pestiferous, Gothic apparition:

> [T]o my diseased fancy, the vessels hurled by him after me, were surcharged with fetid [*sic*] vapour, and my friend's shape, altered by a thousand distortions, expanded into a gigantic phantom, bearing on its brow the sign of pestilence. The growing shadow rose and rose, filling, and then seeming to endeavour to burst beyond, the adamantine vault that bent over, sustaining and enclosing the world.[59]

---

[56] Shelley, *The Last Man*, p. 90.

[57] Shelley, *The Last Man*, p. 94. In a footnote, McWhir explains that the 'veil … invented by Turkish jealousy' is meant to denote a Muslim headdress. William Beckford's Gothic novel *Vathek* (1786) is exemplary of European Orientalism, as its plot follows a Muslim Caliph meddling with supernatural powers.

[58] Shelley, *The Last Man*, pp. 98, 145.   [59] Shelley, *The Last Man*, p. 158.

Much has been said about this phantom Raymond and its potential significance to the novel's political symbolism.[60] But if we read the conquest of Constantinople as the literal enactment of a psychic process, namely that of a self-destructive sympathy with another's suicidal despair, then the phantom Raymond *qua* plague that follows might be read as this very same suicidal despair now unleashed as a virulent social contagion of heightened sympathy and sentimentality. Plague and despair are closely linked in the novel; as Peter Melville rightly notes, 'despair is encoded in both the cause and the effects of infection in *The Last Man*: it is the plague's most effective vehicle of transmission and among its most telling symptoms'.[61] Indeed, Raymond himself blames the plague for a bout of nihilistic despair on the eve of taking Constantinople. No longer interested in rewards or praise for his victories – 'all I ask of Greece is a grave', he laments – Raymond suspects he may have contracted the plague from the surrounding environs and suggests that 'perhaps disease is the real cause of [his] prognostications'. Similarly, it is noted after the plague spreads to England that 'fear and melancholy forebodings were powerful assistants to disease [and] that desponding and brooding care rendered the physical nature of man peculiarly susceptible to infection'.[62] That the plague and despair are closely linked is clear; though we need not go so far perhaps as to state that in *The Last Man* 'the illness plaguing mankind *is* sympathy',[63] a suicidal despair propagated by sympathy is certainly one of the many allegorical resonances encoded in Shelley's depiction of plague in the novel.

The rhetorical use of 'sympathy' to denote the propagation of emotions and ideas analogous to the spread of a contagious disease was well established by the early nineteenth century, and Shelley makes ample use of such rhetoric to portray the spread of mob-like fear in *The Last Man*. In his famous work on *The Sublime and the Beautiful* of 1757, Edmund Burke noted the propensity for emotionally charged language to affect an audience more strongly than simple description:

> We yield to sympathy, what we refuse to description. The truth is, all verbal description, merely as naked description, though never so exact, conveys so poor and insufficient an idea of the thing described, that it could scarcely have the smallest effect, if the speaker did not call in to his aid those modes of speech that mark a strong and lively feeling in himself. Then, by the contagion of our passions, we catch a fire already kindled in another, which probably might never have been struck out by the object described.[64]

---

[60] See Peter Melville, 'The Problem of Immunity in "The Last Man"', *SEL: Studies in English Literature, 1500–1900* 47:4 (Autumn 2007): 825–846 (p. 839); Sterrenburg, 'Anatomy', pp. 337–340; and McWhir, 'Introduction', pp. xxvii–xxxii.

[61] Melville, 'Immunity', p. 839.   [62] Shelley, *The Last Man*, pp. 147, 197.

[63] Deren, 'Revolting Sympathies', p. 144.   [64] Burke, *Sublime and Beautiful*, p. 160.

Some decades later, Shelley's father William Godwin would liken the formation of violent and irrational mobs to a contagious form of sympathy:

> While the sympathy of opinion catches from man to man, especially in numerous meetings, and among persons whose passions have not been used to the curb of judgment, actions may be determined on, which solitary reflection would have rejected. There is nothing more barbarous, cruel and blood-thirsty, than the triumph of a mob.[65]

Shelley uses similar rhetoric to describe mob-like human behaviour in *The Last Man*. Early in the text, Adrian's youthful naivety encourages the aspiring young philosopher to publish his plans for bringing greater equality to the newly Republican England, but the common people, whether unwilling or unable to understand, come to fear Adrian and his progressive politics. To describe the spread of this suspicious fear, Verney relies on language akin to that of Godwin and Burke: 'The feeling was infectious', he notes pithily. Much later in the text and long after the plague's destructive scourge across the globe, Adrian finds himself in competition against a religious zealot for the leadership of the surviving remnant of humanity, and Shelley again blends the language of sympathy and infection to describe the zealot's fear-induced appeal. Another bout of plague triggers a 'contagion of rebellion' such that the 'deluded crowd[s]' become 'miserable prey to their passions' and temporarily choose to support the manipulative zealot over the humanitarian Adrian.[66] These are only two of many examples in the text that demonstrate Shelley's willingness to use the rhetoric of infectious sympathy to describe the spread of emotions or ideas amongst human populations.[67]

In addition to the sympathetic proliferation of emotions or opinions generally, the specific notion of a contagious plague of suicidal despair also had precedent in Shelley's day. It was widely believed and feared that after the publication of Goethe's *The Sorrows of Young Werther* (1774) there occurred an epidemic of copycat suicides. Goethe's novel, a landmark in sentimental literature and a great influence on the early development of Romanticism, follows a series of letters in which the titular character describes his passionate yet ultimately doomed love for a woman who marries an older man; by the end, Werther's despairing passions become too overwhelming, and so the young man shoots himself with a pistol owned by his beloved's husband. Sentimental young readers, so it was believed, identified so strongly with Goethe's deep-feeling

---

[65] Godwin, William, *An Enquiry Concerning Political Justice*, edited by Mark Philp (Oxford: Oxford University Press, 2013), p. 115.
[66] Shelley, *The Last Man*, pp. 34, 314, 317.
[67] For more on Shelley's use of plague and disease as metaphor for revolution, see Sterrenburg.

and sorrowful Werther that they not only took up the fad of dressing like him but of mimicking his suicide as well. Coined the 'Werther Effect' by David Phillips in 1974 but elsewhere called 'Werther-mania' and 'Werther Fever', this epidemic of suicidal contagion supposedly swept through Europe and so thoroughly frightened the authorities that Goethe's novel was banned in many areas.[68] It is debatable whether such an epidemic truly took place,[69] but the notion that it did was certainly commonplace, for later in his life Goethe famously lamented that some of those who read his novel 'thought that they must transform poetry into reality, imitate a novel like this in real life and, in any case, shoot themselves; and what occurred at first among a few took place later among the general public'.[70]

That Shelley was aware of this belief in *Werther*'s potential danger seems likely. Among the many texts Shelley read in 1815 was Germaine de Staël's *On Germany*, in which the author embellishes her account of the German passion for literature by noting that 'Werther has caused more suicides than the most beautiful woman on Earth'.[71] Tellingly, in *Frankenstein* Shelley lists *Werther* as one of the three works read by the creature in his early education, a fact that leads Michelle Faubert to argue that 'the monster appears to become infected with Werther's suicidality'.[72] We know too that Shelley was likely familiar with her mother's association with the figure, for in his introduction to Wollstonecraft's letters to Imlay, which Shelley read in 1815 and reread in 1820, Godwin wrote, 'The following Letters may possibly be found to contain the finest examples of the language of sentiment and passion ever presented to the world. They bear a striking resemblance to the celebrated romance of Werter

---

[68] David P. Phillips, 'The Influence of Suggestion on Suicide: Substantive and Theoretical Implications of the Werther Effect', *American Sociological Review* 39:3 (June 1974): 340–354. For more on *Werther*'s effect on beliefs regarding suicidal contagion during the half century after its publication, see Faubert, '*Werther*', and Lisa Vargo, 'Male and Female Werthers: Romanticism and Gothic Suicide', in William Hughes and Andrew Smith (eds.), *Suicide and the Gothic* (Manchester: Manchester University Press, 2019) pp. 36–51.

[69] See Jan Thorson and Per-Anne Öberg, "Was there a Suicide Epidemic after Goethe's *Werther*?" *Archives of Suicide Research* 7:1 (2003): 69–72; and Menina Mestas, 'The "Werther Effect" of Goethe's *Werther*: Anecdotal Evidence in Historical News Reports', *Health Communication* (2023): 1–6.

[70] Quoted in Faubert, '*Werther*', p. 408.

[71] My translation. Original: 'Werther a causé plus de suicides que la plus belle femme du monde'. Germaine de Staël, *De L'Allemagne*, 3 vols (Paris: 1813), vol. 1, p. 238. www.gutenberg.org/cache/epub/66924/pg66924-images.html [last Accessed 16 August 2023]. Reference to works read by Shelley here and later in this paragraph taken from Mary Shelley, *The Journals of Mary Shelley, 1814–1844*, edited by Paula R. Feldman and Diana Scott-Kilvert, 2 Vols (Oxford: Clarendon Press; New York: Oxford University Press, 1987). www.nlx.com/collections/110 [last accessed 16 August 2023].

[72] Faubert, 'Challenging Sympathy', p. 321.

[*sic*]'.[73] Godwin doubled down on this association, calling Wollstonecraft a 'Female Werter [*sic*]' in his *Memoirs of the Author of a* Vindication of the Rights of Woman.[74] One might even surmise that Shelley too thought of herself as something of a 'female Werther' during the years she wrote *The Last Man*. It is well known that in the years following Percy's death Shelley identified with the lonely character that would eventually serve as the narrator for her post-apocalyptic epic. 'The last man!' Shelley writes in her journal in May of 1824, '[y]es, I may well describe that solitary being's feelings, feeling myself as the last relic of a beloved race, my companions, extinct before me'. Though Shelley does not make a similarly explicit identification with Werther in her 'Journal of Sorrow' – as is the title given to her journal covering the years between Percy's death and the publication of *The Last Man* – Shelley nonetheless resembles such a character in her repeated 'praye[rs] . . . for death' in the wake of the loss of her husband. Just as Werther could not bear the thought of living without his beloved, so too does Shelley long to join Percey in the grave 'beneath that weed grown tower' and come to 'underst[and] the feelings that le[a]d to suicide'.[75]

One can only speculate as to what extent *Werther* might have been on Shelley's mind as she composed *The Last Man*; nonetheless, something like 'Werther-mania' is inscribed in the events of the text in two significant ways. First, the despairing susceptibility to the plague, much like *Werther*'s purport-edly fatal sentimentality, travels contagiously via the written word. In her study on contagionist versus anti-contagionist rhetoric in *The Last Man*, Anne McWhir notes that Shelley's novel evinces support for 'contingent contagion-ism', a position held by many of Shelley's contemporaries that maintained 'disease could be transmitted through contact given certain atmospheric condi-tions and a certain susceptibility in the victim'.[76] As proof, McWhir quotes Verney, who claims that 'bodies are sometimes in a state to reject the infection of malady, and at others, thirsty to imbibe it'.[77] As has already been noted, fear and despair are significant causes of such susceptibility, and the novel suggests that this emotion-induced susceptibility can itself be propagated by the printed word. As the plague begins to spread in England, Verney notes that Adrian worked 'to disguise the symptoms and progress of the plague' for he 'knew that fear and melancholy forebodings were powerful assistants to disease'.

---

[73] William Godwin, *Posthumous Works of the Author of a Vindication of the Rights of Woman*, 4 Vols (London: 1798), vol. 3, p. iii. www.gutenberg.org/cache/epub/23233/pg23233-images.html [last accessed 16 August 2023].

[74] Quoted in Michelle Faubert, 'The Fictional Suicides of Mary Wollstonecraft', *Literature Compass* 12:12 (2015): 652–659 (p. 653).

[75] Shelley, *The Journals*, pp. 476–477, 475, 474, 486.

[76] McWhir, 'Anti-Contagionism', p. 26.

[77] Shelley, *The Last Man*, pp. 182–83; quoted in McWhir, 'Anti-Contagionism', p. 25.

His endeavour comes late, however, for the susceptibility of the plague had already been incited by news of the plague's arrival:

> At length it was mentioned in the newspapers.... Before it had been a rumour; but now in words uneraseable, in definite and undeniable print, the knowledge went forth. Its obscurity of situation rendered it the more conspicuous: the diminutive letters grew gigantic to the bewildered eye of fear.[78]

About this passage, McWhir states, '[t]he word [plague] alone ... is a metaphor made flesh, for the word carries the plague across channels and boundaries to infect the world'.[79] Earlier, a conversation within Verney's circle on the likelihood of instituting a utopian paradise on earth is cut short by Verney's reading aloud a newspaper article on the plague's spread through Greece. Commenting on this event, Verney recounts, '[t]his intelligence brought us back from the prospect of paradise ... to the pain and misery at present existent on earth'.[80] The despair incited by news of the plague can thus neuter utopian optimism and make those present susceptible to the very plague about which they speak. McWhir puts it pithily – in the novel, '*plague* is a killing word'.[81] In sum, reading about the plague makes it more likely one might contract the plague, much as those fearing the spread of suicidal contagion believed *Werther* might propagate its own contagious despair.

Secondly, and somewhat more abstractly, we can return again to the relationship between the two halves of the text, reading the first half as the *Werther*-esque sentimental tragedy that, with its conclusion in the precise midpoint of the text, unleashes an unstoppable effluvial despair that suffuses and dominates the novel's second half. Though Shelley, as we have seen, incorporates elements of 'contingent contagionism' into her depiction of plague in the novel, McWhir demonstrates nonetheless that *The Last Man* falls more firmly on the side of an anti-contagionist position. One must be careful to avoid the simple anachronism of using contemporary understandings of bacterial and viral contagion to discuss the plague depicted in *The Last Man*, for as McWhir notes, the early nineteenth century saw a debate over two competing theories of disease transmission:

> the contagionist views that underlay quarantine laws and that were based on the belief in a particular source of infection – the *contagium vivum* – transmitted by contact or body fluids; and 'anti-contagionism,' which located the source of disease in a quality of the air itself, often a 'miasma' generated in particular but remote places and carried on the winds.[82]

---

[78] Shelley, *The Last Man*, pp. 187, 186.   [79] McWhir, 'Anti-Contagionism', p. 34.
[80] Shelley, *The Last Man*, p. 173.   [81] McWhir, 'Anti-Contagionism', p. 34.
[82] McWhir, 'Anti-Contagionism', p. 23.

Verney expresses a confident belief in the views of the latter camp: 'that the plague was not what is commonly called contagious, like the scarlet fever, or extinct small-pox, was proved'.[83] McWhir is likely justified in noting that Verney's expression here reflects Shelley's own anti-contagionist position,[84] but even were we tempted to question Verney's reliability, Shelley's depiction of the plague suggests that the malady is indeed caused by 'air . . . subject to infection' blown unstoppably across the national borders of Europe, for the plague is barely slowed let alone halted by 'strict quarantine[s]' like that enacted at Thessaly early in its spread.[85]

This effluvial or miasmatic air is itself analogous to a contractible form of despair permeating the very air one breathes. We have seen already that Raymond suspects that his nihilistic musings upon death are the result of breathing in the plagued air of Constantinople, but Shelley most explicitly muddles the distinction between physical and emotional ailments in an extended scene that takes Verney through three landmarks in the presently plague-infested London. Finding despair and suffering in each of the three locations, Verney can tellingly find reprieve only in the thought of clean air. He first visits St. Bartholomew's Hospital. Witnessing the scores of those suffering from the plague, Verney notes, '[t]he ward was filled with an effluvia that caused my heart to heave with painful qualms'. His reaction to the hospital's air is ambiguous, as a 'heaving heart' can be read as both a physical effect and a figurative description of his emotional state. Verney then leaves the hospital 'distracted by painful emotions' and attempts to take his mind off such emotions by fantasising about the open countryside, which 'affords no such mass of horrors'. Next, Verney stumbles into Drury Lane Theatre and finds a rendition of *Macbeth* already in progress. For a while, the fantasy serves as escapism to take the audience away from the horrors outside the theatre; that is, until the events of the play begin to reflect reality. As Macduff expresses theatrical grief at the loss of his family, the crowd, suffering from 'high wrought sympathy', feels this painful loss as their own: 'A pang of tameless grief wrenched every heart, a burst of despair was echoed from every lip – I had entered into the universal feeling – I had been absorbed by the terrors of Rosse – I re-echoed the cry of Macduff'. Here, the 'mist that floated about' the stage is no longer a phantasmal screen rendering forms 'frightful, unreal and fanciful'; rather, it becomes akin to the effluvial air of the plague. Everyone inside the theatre is steeped in the mire of shared despair, and thus Verney once again escapes 'to find calm in the free air and silent street'. Finally, Verney stumbles

---

[83] Shelley, *The Last Man*, p. 182.   [84] McWhir, 'Anti-Contagionism', p. 25.
[85] Shelley, *The Last Man*, pp. 182, 173.

into Westminster Abbey and tries to take solace in sympathetic community. Though he finds peace and calm initially in 'the sight of many other human creatures offering up prayers and submission', this feeling does not last, for the sudden death of one of the choristers shatters this sympathetic image and reveals that even upon holy grounds one is vulnerable. Once again, Verney finds solace only upon escaping from the enclosed and intimate company of others: '[i]n the open air alone I found relief'.[86] It is thus as if the events at Constantinople literalise the emotional fallout of the sentimental tragedy and infuse it into the surrounding environment. Sympathy transforms from the localised to the omnipresent, from an epidemic of contagious passions to a pandemic of effluvial despair. The process of taking in another's emotional suffering is made material, literalised and embodied in the act of breathing in the despair shared by all.

2.3 'They Looked at Me with Unsympathetic Complacency'

Though we have spent much time considering sympathy in Shelley's *The Last Man*, our discussion has thus far overlooked the novel's portrayal of Verney after he finally becomes the titular character. Though he does over the course of his narration include the odd interjection noting his solitary present, Verney reserves the bulk of his account of being the Last Man for the final (roughly) five percent of the novel. Without other humans with whom to interact and sympathise, Verney may be spared the infectious despair that marked the previous sections, but a despair that stems from a profound lack of sympathy nonetheless characterises Verney's closing narration. Though he holds out hope that he might find another human being with whom to sympathise, Verney *qua* Last Man ultimately confronts a world of unsympathetic indifference. Whereas Verney had earlier fled the sympathetically threatening crowds of Bartholomew's Hospital, Drury Lane Theatre, and Westminster Abbey by escaping into 'the free air and silent street', here the terminally solitary Verney laments that he cannot escape the dreadful silence of the 'abyss of the present'.[87]

Not for lack of trying does Verney find himself without sympathy, for he attempts in vain to find the companionship he craves in both the creatures of nature and the lifeless products of human culture. Since the creatures of the natural world still thrive having been spared the ravages of the plague, to those creatures Verney vows to 'discipline my sorrowing heart to sympathy in your joys' and to 'be happy, because ye are so'. In a proto-Darwinian acknowledgement of humankind's continuity and kinship with nature, Verney goes so far as to state, 'I am not much unlike you. Nerves, pulse, brain, joint, and flesh, of such am I composed, and ye are organized by the same laws'. But his new philosophy

---

[86] Shelley, *The Last Man*, pp. 219–222. [87] Shelley, *The Last Man*, pp. 221, 361.

fails its very first test, for Verney is rebuked by a family of goats when he attempts to befriend them. Enraged by this rejection, he declares that he 'will not live among the wild scenes of nature'. Giving up on sympathy with the natural world, Verney sets out to 'seek the towns – Rome, the capital of the world, the crown of man's achievements'. Yet here too he finds only unsympathetic indifference to his plight. Though he continues to seek out other survivors, Verney looks also to find consolation in what he regards as the artefacts of humankind's cultural pinnacle, Rome's 'storied streets, hallowed ruins, and stupendous remains of human exertion', for he notes that 'the voice of dead time, in still vibrations, is breathed from these dumb things, animated and glorified as they were by man'. As it was with the unsympathetic goats, however, Verney's almost pantheistic vision of sympathy with the remains of human culture is quickly dashed:

> [I] stood surrounded by marble forms of divine beauty. Each stone deity was possessed by sacred gladness, and the eternal fruition of love. They looked at me with unsympathetic complacency, and often in wild accents I reproached them for their supreme indifference – for they were human shapes, the human form divine was manifest in each fairest limb and lineament.[88]

Verney describes objects that are in some sense 'perfect' humans, exquisite instantiations of a Platonic Ideal, and yet, lacking any animal vitalism, these forms remain but cold and lifeless abstractions. As a result of these dual failures to find sympathy, for quite some time Verney remains completely and abysmally alone, the creations of both nature and human culture indifferent to his suffering.

Verney is too human, participates too much in the 'human form divine', to find sympathetic companionship amongst animals, but he is also too animal, too much of the animal body and its passions, to find a satisfactory sympathetic companionship amongst the Platonic ideality of the artistic products of human culture. Such is Shelley's schematic of sympathy: on either end of the spectrum sit the 'embodied animal' and the 'abstract human', respectively, and only within a window at the midpoint of this spectrum do we find 'humanity', which is to say the living human being and its sympathies. In other words, the human being, for Shelley, does not fall on the obvious side of a human/animal binary but is rather a site of hybridity and liminality, a compromise between the 'embodied animal' *qua* instinct/passion/body and the 'abstract human' *qua* culture/reason/mind. This understanding of sympathy lends insight into Verney's only successful attempt at finding sympathetic companionship after becoming the Last Man: that with a shepherd's dog, whom Verney discovers

[88] Shelley, *The Last Man*, pp. 358–359, 363.

still 'tending sheep … fulfilling his duties in expectation of his [master's] return'. Like Verney, the dog feels animal emotions and passions, showing 'delight' and 'boisterous gratitude' when Verney engages with it. But also like Verney, the dog is too much conditioned by human culture to fit in with nature, for his habitual rehearsal of his role as shepherd dog – 'his repetition of lessons learned from man, now useless, though unforgotten' – evince his deep-seated alignment with human culture.[89] Shelley in a sense pre-emptively criticises the likes of Derrida and Haraway, for whereas the latter philosophers use domesticated animals such as cats and dogs as sites for 'propos[ing] new kinds of posthuman sympathy dedicated to radical otherness',[90] Shelley questions just how radical the sympathy with a domesticated animal can be. By juxtaposing the immediate love of the domesticated dog with the suspicion of the wild goat, Shelley carves out a space for a notion of humanity *qua* sympathy that includes the cultural product of the domesticated dog. But though they are both products of human culture, the domesticated dog is also of a different order than that of the unsympathetic statue, for there is no trace of the animal in the latter. 'Humanity', therefore, must be both animal and cultural, a point of compromise between the 'embodied animal' and the 'abstract human', and it is only here, suggests Shelley, that true sympathetic relationships can reside.[91]

But let us not forget, that for Shelley the true sympathetic relationship is not strictly beneficial or benign, to which the dangerous and despairing sympathies of the bulk of the narrative attest. Verney himself expresses his own sympathetically suicidal fantasies when, after entering his final solitude, he reflects on the deaths of Adrian and Idris: 'I would have wound myself like ivy inextricably round them, so that the same blow might destroy us. I would have entered and been a part of them – so that "[i]f the dull substance of my flesh were thought", even now I had accompanied them to their new and incommunicable abode'.[92] As it was with Perdita, so it is with Verney; both crave another's sympathy to the

---

[89] Shelley, *The Last Man*, p. 365.

[90] Elisabeth Arnould-Bloomfield, 'Posthuman Compassions', *PMLA* 130:5 (2015): 1467–1475 (p. 1468).

[91] This argument runs counter to that of some recent ecocritical readings of the text which either read Verney as returning to a state of animality in his closing narration or read Shelley as critiquing the anthropocentrism of the human/animal binary by collapsing it in favour of something akin to Deep Ecology. For the former, see Andrea Haslanger, 'The Last Animal: Cosmopolitanism in *The Last Man*', *European Romantic Review* 27:5 (2016): 659–678; for the latter, see Lauren Cameron, 'Questioning Agency: Dehumanizing Sustainability in Mary Shelley's *The Last Man*', in Ben P. Robertson (ed.), *Romantic Sustainability: Endurance and the Natural World, 1780–1830* (Maryland: Lexington Books, 2016), pp. 261–273.

[92] Shelley, *The Last Man*, p. 352. According to McWhir's notes, Shelley quotes here from Shakespeare's Sonnet 44.

point of the obliteration of their own Self. Or, to add to Sartre's famous quip –
Hell is other people, but so too is abject solitude.

For Rebecca Richardson, the blurring of the '"natural" and "manmade"
worlds' in *The Last Man* contribute to what she calls the 'environmental
uncanny'.[93] We might add an additional Gothic resonance to this blurred
binary – the monster. As Jeffrey Jerome Cohen states, the monster is characterised by a 'refusal to participate in the classificatory "order of things"', for 'they
are disturbing hybrids … a form suspended between forms that threatens to
smash distinctions'.[94] Fitting in neither amongst the purely natural animal
world nor the lifeless remains of cultural production, torn between the world
of the living (animal) and the dead (abstraction), pining for a sympathetic
merger with the Other that is in fact a wish for the obliteration of Self –
Verney thus becomes a lone and lonely monster akin to the creature of
Frankenstein. What's more, Shelley reveals, as all Gothic authors do to some
extent, that the human being is always-already monstrous, for it is by definition
a hybrid of the 'embodied animal' and the 'abstract human', one that seeks out
sympathetic – and thus painful, despairing, and sometimes fatal – mergers with
others. This 'monstrification'[95] of the human, as we shall see, is a defining
feature not only of Shelley's *The Last Man*, but of *The Time Machine* and *I Am
Legend* as well.

3 Wells's Vicious Sympathy

If Shelley describes a Last Man adrift between two poles of unsympathetic
indifference, it will be H. G. Wells who first gives us a Last Man who must
confront the inverse of such indifference – predatory interest. Like its counterpart, predatory interest has both its 'embodied animal' and 'abstract human'
poles. The former, rather self-explanatory, is the focused gaze of the animal
predator as it stalks its prey; by the latter, I have in mind the stereotype of the
cold, calculating man or machine of Reason that hunts, dissects and destroys out
of a purely callous interest in learning about its object: the worst stereotype of
the Victorian vivisectionist, for instance, or the calm and calculating killer robot
of the modern Dystopia. In both cases, predation models a perverse form of
sympathy: the Other is absorbed completely by the Self, whether captured
orally or ocularly, whether digested or dissected. There is something predatory,
to be sure, in the sympathetic conquests of both Lord Raymond and the plague,

---

[93] Rebecca Richardson, 'The Environmental Uncanny: Imagining the Anthropocene in Mary
Shelley's *The Last Man*', *ISLE: Interdisciplinary Studies in Literature and Environment* 26:4
(Autumn 2019): pp. 1062–1083 (pp. 1072–1073).
[94] Cohen, 'Monster Culture', p. 45.
[95] Koenig-Woodyard, 'The Mathematics of Monstrosity', p. 85.

but the immediate solitary experience of Shelley's Last Man is characterised entirely by unsympathetic indifference only. It is rather odd, in fact, that Verney faces no animal predation once he finds himself alone in the world. In a Rome now almost completely devoid of human life, non-human animals such as sheep and buffalo may roam freely, but these animals pose no reported threat to Verney and are instead completely indifferent to his presence. One could easily imagine Shelley invoking the symbolism of the wolf returning to prowl the city that myth claims it helped to found, but Shelley makes no such invocation. Considering the other side of the spectrum, it is perhaps not as easy to imagine Shelley opting to threaten Verney's solitude with something akin to the mechanical humanoids of the *Terminator* franchise. Of course, in many ways Shelley's *Frankenstein* is a forebearer of this very trope, but to expect something similar from the lifeless marble statues of Verney's Rome would be highly anachronistic. Regardless, Shelley's Last Man ultimately finds himself in a beautiful yet empty Eden, one that is without threat only because it is utterly indifferent to him.

Wells's Last Man, the Traveller of *The Time Machine*, finds himself in a world that appears at first glance to be much like that of Verney's Rome. On its first impression, London of the year 802 701 appears to be a calm and pleasant garden, devoid of disease and predation. Populating the otherwise empty palaces interspersed among this garden are the Eloi, descendants of a decadent humanity that have devolved in both physical stature and intelligence. Though they demonstrate mild curiosity towards the Traveller at first, ultimately the Eloi prove to be more akin to the indifferent animals and statues of Verney's world. The Traveller makes particular note of the Eloi's 'lack of interest' – 'They would come to me with eager cries of astonishment, like children, but, like children, they would soon stop examining me, and wander away after some other toy'. The only exception to this Eloi indifference is Weena, with whom the Traveller 'carr[ies] on a miniature flirtation'. Notable here are the circumstances that incite such a relationship, for the Traveller saves Weena from drowning after it becomes clear that none of her fellow Eloi intend on 'ma[king] the slightest attempt to rescue the weakly-crying little thing which was drowning before their eyes'. Weena's attachment to the Traveller, then, is more a consequence of the Eloi's natural sympathetic indifference then it is evidence of a widespread proclivity among the Eloi toward amorous forms of emotional attachment. A few more similarities of note between the Eloi and that of Verney's world – like the unsympathetic goats of Shelley's *The Last Man*, the Eloi are also 'strict vegetarians'; like the statues of Verney's Rome, the Eloi are described as possessing a 'Dresden china type of prettiness', thus aligning them with the Platonic ideality of the statue.[96] Ultimately, the surface world of Wells's future London at once models an Edenic return to a Rousseauian 'State of Nature' and a techno-Utopian state of statuesque perfection, one wherein the removal of all strife and necessity leaves behind an unsympathetic indifference.

But lurking beneath this idealised vision of a beautiful if indifferent London are the Gothic vestiges of the predatory instinct. The Traveller comes to discover that the Eloi are not the only descendants of the human species, for the subterranean Morlocks come up to the surface at night to feed on their evolutionary cousins. While the Eloi might embody the Romantic notion of nature as a sublime and peaceful harmony, the Morlocks reflect the post-Darwinian paradigm, one that had adopted as axioms Darwin's 'war of nature', Tennyson's 'nature, red in tooth and claw', and Spencer's 'survival of the fittest'.[97] Foreshadowing this transformation from polished indifference to bestial predation is the statue of the sphinx that welcomes the Traveller to the future London, for though we might suspect that this inanimate form should align itself with the indifference of Shelley's statues, instead the Traveller notes something sinister in the sphinx's gaze: 'the sightless eyes seemed to watch me; there was the faint shadow of a smile on the lips'.[98] Just as the Eloi were indicative of both the 'embodied animal' and 'abstract human' poles of the spectrum of unsympathetic indifference, so too are the Morlocks indicative of both poles of predatory interest. In addition to being described in distinctly bestial and animalistically predatory terms, the Morlocks are repeatedly aligned with machines and mechanism. 'Their minds were essentially mechanical', notes the Traveller in an early version of the novel, serialised in the *National Observer* in 1894.[99] Furthermore, as I will demonstrate in this section, the Morlocks are also metaphorically linked to the callous inquisitiveness of the late-Victorian vivisectionist, for there is some evidence to suggest that these creatures are interested in understanding the mechanism of physiology as much as they are that of technology.

Given the aforementioned, one might suspect that there would be little mention of sympathy from Wells's Traveller, as he finds only unsympathetic indifference from the Eloi and predatory interest from the Morlocks. In many ways, the companionship the Traveller finds in Weena is far more like that which Verney finds in the shepherd's dog than in another human companion,

[96] H. G. Wells, *The Time Machine*, edited by Nicholas Ruddick (Peterborough: Broadview Press, 2001), pp. 87, 103, 85, 82.
[97] Though many ascribe 'survival of the fittest' to Darwin, it was in fact in his 1864 *Principles of Biology* that Herbert Spencer coined the phrase.
[98] Wells, *Time Machine*, p. 80.
[99] Robert M. Philmus and David Y. Hughes (eds.), *H. G. Wells: Early Writings in Science and Science Fiction* (California: University of California Press, 1975), p. 87.

and thus the Traveller's situation seems to mimic that of Verney quite closely. And yet, the Traveller notes more than once that he not only feels a kind of companionship with Weena but also that he feels sympathy for the Eloi in general, a sympathy that is at once an instinctively empathic response to the Eloi's appearance and an active feeling of pity for their lowly fate. By siding emotionally with the Eloi against their more bestial cousins, the Traveller sets up a complicated and richly layered sympathetic relationship. On one level, the Traveller's instinctive sympathies for the creature that appears *more human* evinces a deep-seated bias against living beings that we tend to see as danger-ous, as pests and as vermin; on another level, the Traveller's sympathies are in fact aligned with the *less human* of the two future descendants of humanity. Scholarship tends to read both the Morlocks and the Eloi in terms of human degeneration and retrogression, and not without reason.[100] However, as I will demonstrate in this section, the Morlock/Eloi relationship also figures analo-gous relationships both between the human consumer and their livestock and between the human vivisectionist and their animal specimen. By painting the Morlock in such disgust-inducing terms, Wells in essence defamiliarises the human being and allows the Traveller to more easily share in the experience of animals fated for the dinner plate and the dissection table. But before we think to champion Wells as an early proponent for animal rights, the truly Gothic twist will prove to be the fickle and ultimately impotent power of these sympathies: for Wells, sympathy with the non-human animal is little more than an exercise in masochistic voyeurism, a titillating glimpse into the horrors of a natural world that humankind has only temporarily escaped.

3.1 'They Had Kept Too Much of Their Human Form'

In *The Logic of Fantasy*, John Huntington highlights that though 'the touch of the Morlocks is hardly distinguishable from that of the Eloi', the Traveller reacts very differently to these two respective actions: 'When he first meets the Eloi he allows them to touch him.... Similar behaviour by the Morlocks, however, leads the Time Traveller to an hysterical smashing of skulls'.[101] Huntington's point is premised on the Traveller's use of distinctly inhuman metaphors to describe the initial touch of both these creatures. When the first crowd of Eloi

---

[100] See William Greenslade, *Degeneration, Culture and the Novel 1880–1940* (Cambridge: Cambridge University Press, 1994), pp. 38–39; Daniel Pick, *Faces of Degeneration: A European Disorder, c. 1848 – c. 1918* (Cambridge: Cambridge University Press, 1989); pp. 157–159; Chapter 2 of Steven McLean, *The Early Fiction of H. G. Wells: Fantasies of Science* (New York: Palgrave Macmillan, 2009); and Hurley, *Gothic Body*, pp. 79–88.

[101] John Huntington, *The Logic of Fantasy: H. G. Wells and Science Fiction* (New York: Columbia University Press, 1982), p. 44.

show their initial, if quickly waning curiosity towards him, the Traveller notes, 'I felt . . . soft little tentacles upon my back and shoulders'.[102] Some time later, the Traveller describes a disturbing dream in which 'sea-anemones were feeling over [his] face with their soft palps'; he then 'w[akes] with a start, and with an odd fancy that some greyish animal had just rushed out of the chamber'.[103] At this point in his narration, the Traveller has yet to learn the identity of these 'greyish animal[s]', but once he does, he 'shudder[s] with horror to think how [the Morlocks] must have examined [him]' while he slept.[104] Compare this feeling of horror to his expression of casual disregard at the Eloi's own examination of him: 'They wanted to make sure I was real. There was nothing in this all that alarming'.[105] The Eloi's inquisitive 'tentacles' are not at all alarming, whereas the Morlocks's 'soft palps' are worthy of shuddering horror. We can add to Huntington's observation that both descriptions foreshadow the Traveller's encounter with the 'monster crab' millions of years farther into the future: 'I felt a tickling on my cheek as though a fly had lighted there . . . With a frightful qualm, I turned, and saw that I had grasped the antenna of another monster crab that stood just behind me'. Again, touch is here described in terms of an appendage that is not only inhuman but distinctly non-simian and non-mammalian, and as with the touch of the Morlocks, the Traveller's impulse is to attribute carnivorous malice to this touch, for he recounts, '[i]ts evil eyes were wriggling on their stalks, its mouth was alive with appetite'.[106]

Tentacles, palps, antenna – three similarly inquisitive appendages, yet only two of the three elicit an abject response. What are we to make of this discrepancy? The obvious explanation is that whereas he feels threatened when in the presence of the Morlocks and the giant crab, the Traveller does not feel that the Eloi present the same danger. '[T]hey looked so frail', after all, that the Traveller can imagine himself 'flinging . . . them about like nine-pins'. Yet the Morlocks are similarly weak in comparison to the Traveller: they are 'smaller and lighter' than he is; their hands, like those of the Eloi, are more than once described as 'soft'; and they injure easily, for when describing his penultimate confrontation with the creatures, the Traveller describes feeling 'bones grind under the blow of [his] fist' and 'the succulent giving of flesh and bone under [his] blows'. Nor does this explanation account for why the Traveller '[i]nstinctively . . . loathe[s] them' and comes to 'long[] very much to kill a Morlock'. This is not to say that the Traveller feels no threat from the Morlocks, for he eventually admits to feeling 'like a beast in a trap, whose

---

[102] Wells, *Time Machine*, p. 82; quoted in Huntington, p. 44.

[103] Wells, *Time Machine*, p. 104; partially quoted in Huntington, p. 44.

[104] Wells, *Time Machine*, p. 120.   [105] Wells, *Time Machine*, p. 82; quoted in Huntington, p. 44.

[106] Wells, *Time Machine*, p. 146.

enemy would come upon him soon'.[107] Yet clearly there is something psychologically deeper at work here. That his instinctive and abject repulsion is felt before the Morlocks pose any obvious threat to him proves that such repulsion goes beyond a simple sense of self-preservation.

What, then, explains the Traveller's 'peculiar shrinking from those pallid bodies'? The Traveller gives his own explanation: 'Probably my shrinking was largely due to the sympathetic influence of the Eloi, whose disgust of the Morlocks I now began to appreciate'. Notably, the Traveller begins to understand this disgust before he learns that the Morlocks in fact feed upon the Eloi; at present, he only has the revolting visage of the Morlocks to explain the Eloi's disgust, yet the Morlocks' ugliness is enough for him to justify his own sympathetic agreement with the Eloi. After he learns that the Eloi have in fact become prey to those they had once subjugated and driven underground, the Traveller reflects upon the nonetheless persistent power of these creatures' sympathetic influence:

> I tried to preserve myself from the horror that was coming upon me, by regarding it as a rigorous punishment of human selfishness. Man had been content to live in ease and delight upon the labours of his fellow-man, had taken Necessity as his watchword and excuse, and in the fulness [*sic*] of time Necessity had come home to him. I even tried a Carlyle-like scorn of this wretched aristocracy-in-decay. But this attitude of mine was impossible. However great their intellectual degradation, the Eloi had kept too much of their human form not to claim my sympathy, and to make me perforce a sharer in their degradation and their Fear.[108]

Here, sympathy trumps any attempt to reason through the facts of the situation, as the Traveller is unable to feel otherwise than what his sympathies compel him to feel. Though their tentacle-like touch hints at their evolutionary distance from their human ancestors, the Eloi are nonetheless too ostensibly 'human' such that their image cannot help but belie their inhuman reality.

As for the Morlocks, the Time Traveller proves that he is incapable of sympathy with, or perhaps unwilling to extend sympathy to, creatures that lack phenotypic similarity with the human being. The closest he gets to sympathising with the Morlocks is during the previously quoted attempt to look at the Eloi's state as a form of punishment, but even here he cannot bring himself to feel anything for the ugly Morlocks beside contempt for 'these inhuman sons of men'.[109] The direct cause of his abject response seems to be a form of what Ernest Small calls 'biophobia'. In his two part article on the challenges faced by

---

[107] Wells, *Time Machine*, pp. 82, 114, 115, 136, 137, 119, 130, 119.
[108] Wells, *Time Machine*, pp. 113, 125.   [109] Wells, *Time Machine*, p. 125.

wildlife conservation agencies to secure public interest and funding, Small considers how the tendency for people to be biophobic, 'i.e. slightly to extremely negative towards the majority of species they encounter', limits the number of species that can garner support for conservation.[110] Small gives an extensive list of unattractive animal features that can dissuade human interest or affection for an animal, and it is perhaps unsurprising that many of these features are similarly characteristic of the Morlocks:

> Competitor for resources or preys on humans, livestock, or damages crops (predators, parasites, pests, vermin) . . .
> Quite unlike human form: 'creepy-crawlies', 'bugs', 'worms' . . .
> Possession of human-like features that appear unhealthy, aged, or diseased and provoke urge for avoidance . . .
> Clumsy, slow, or erratic movements . . .
> Lives in earth, mud, or inside other species
> Not viewable (shy, nocturnal, 'sneaky', or lives below ground or in the sea . . .)
> Poikilothermy ('cold-blooded'; temperature mostly determined by environment).[111]

Compare this list to the various descriptions and names the Traveller gives to the Morlocks: he calls the first one he sees a 'human spider', a 'little monster' and a 'bleached, obscene, nocturnal Thing'; he then calls the Morlock species 'this new vermin' after noting they are 'filthily cold to the touch' and are 'the half-bleached colour of the worms and things one sees preserved in spirit in a zoological museum'; he compares their big eyes to those of the 'abysmal fishes' and calls them 'nauseatingly inhuman' on account of their 'pale, chinless faces and great, lidless, pinkish-grey eyes'; he twice compares the Morlocks to ants, once by calling them 'ant-like' and once while imagining them underground 'on their ant-hill going hither and thither'; finally, the Traveller calls them 'human rats' during a confrontation in which he can feel their 'little teeth nipping at [his] neck'.[112] Put simply, if the Morlocks were an endangered species, they would likely garner no public support.

On the surface, then, *The Time Machine* seems to argue that human biases will inevitably shape our sympathetic relationships with ostensibly non-human or starkly inhuman beings. Sympathetic relations in the novel seem so heavily weighted toward the human form and away from the ostensibly bestial that one might be tempted to suggest that the text's exploration of the nature of sympathy is one of the least Gothic aspects of what is otherwise an undoubtedly Gothic

---

[110] Ernest Small, 'The New Noah's Ark: Beautiful and Useful Species Only. Part 1. Biodiversity Conservation Issues and Priorities', *Biodiversity* 12:4 (2011): 232–247 (p. 233).

[111] Ernest Small, 'The New Noah's Ark: Beautiful and Useful Species Only. Part 2. The Chosen Species', *Biodiversity* 13:1 (2012): 37–53 (p. 38).

[112] Wells, *Time Machine*, pp. 107, 113, 115, 117, 125, 122, 137.

text. But as it was with the Traveller's impressions of London in the year 802 701, what appears to be true on the surface does not reflect the truth of the depths. Though the Traveller clearly regards the Morlocks as the less human of the two species – 'the modification of the human type', he notes at one point, 'was even more profound than among the Eloi'[113] – such a judgement is premised upon what Huntington calls 'a symmetrical illusion: the Eloi, because of their appearance, seem more human than they are; the Morlocks, again because of their appearance, seem less'.[114] Because of this illusion, the Traveller does not openly recognise that he 'bears far less resemblance to the mild, effeminate [Eloi] than to the Morlocks'. This observation comes from Kelly Hurley, who in *The Gothic Body* thoroughly elaborates on these resemblances:

> For in contrast to their apish appearance, the Morlocks are exemplary Victorians: they are intelligent, shrewd, and industrious; they operate complex machinery; they are actively employed in the production of useful goods. They are energetically masculine, like the Time Traveller himself. . . . And finally, they are white: the raciality of the Eloi is not particularly foregrounded, but the Morlocks' most emphatically is.[115]

All this being true, the Traveller's sympathies might thus be far more radical than they first appear, for by aligning his sympathies with the Eloi, the Traveller sympathises with the species that is in fact the least human of the two (at least from the ideological standpoint of the Victorian gentleman). As I will demonstrate, the relationship between the Morlocks and the Eloi can thus be read as a defamiliarised reflection on the relationships between the human consumer and its butchered livestock and between the vivisectionist and its animal subjects. Put another way, the Gothic core of Wells's sympathetic imaginary is in its proto-Deleuzian explorations into *becoming*-prey and *becoming*-specimen.

3.2 'Prejudice against Human Flesh Is No Deep Seated-Instinct'

As already noted, the Morlocks figure both the 'embodied animal' and the 'abstract human' poles of the spectrum of predatory interest, both the carnivorous hunger to feed on and the callous interest in the dissection of other beings. The former is the most obviously apparent, as the Morlocks' carnivorous nature is explicitly foregrounded in the text. The Traveller's first clear sign that predation has in fact survived to the year 802 701 is given to him during his foray into the Morlocks' underground lair. By the aid of a lit match, the

---

[113] Wells, *Time Machine*, p. 111.   [114] Huntington, *Fantasy*, p. 44.
[115] Hurley, *Gothic Body*, p. 87.

Traveller peers into the Morlocks' dark abode and discovers a table, 'laid with what seemed a meal'. The Traveller gives no description of this meal besides the hunk of meat, the 'red joint' as he calls it, lying on the table, yet with this evidence alone the Traveller deduces that the Morlocks, unlike their vegetarian cousins, are carnivorous. It is only a short time later that the Traveller further deduces that the meat on the table was likely that of an Eloi, and thus the Traveller concludes, the 'Eloi were mere fatted cattle, which the ant-like Morlocks preserved and preyed upon – probably saw to the breeding of'. As is well known, however, the Traveller charges the Morlocks not with animal husbandry but with cannibalism – '[the] prejudice against human flesh is no deep seated-instinct', he muses before exclaiming, '[a]nd so these inhuman sons of men–!'[116] The Traveller may not finish the thought, but this abrupt silence just elevates the horror, for as Hurley notes, 'cannibalism [here] is the great unspeakable'.[117] The Traveller then follows up with a more explicit reference, comparing the Morlocks to 'our cannibal ancestors of three or four thousand years ago'. Though he notes that these future humanoids 'were less human and more remote' than these cannibal ancestors, the implication nonetheless is that the Morlocks' feeding on the Eloi is overdetermined with cannibalistic excess.[118]

And yet, the Traveller (and perhaps Wells himself) gets his allegory mixed up with his scientific speculation. As a political allegory for the lower classes rising up against the upper class, the charge of cannibalism fits well enough, though Kathryn Hume is right to criticise the imagery given that it is the 'Haves' who 'normally exploit, "eat", or consume Have-nots in a capitalist system'.[119] Diegetically, however, the Traveller's accusation of cannibalism does not hold water, as even he diagnoses this future world as one in which 'Man had not remained one species, but had differentiated into two distinct animals'.[120] His use of the words 'species' and 'animal' instead of the more ambiguous and loaded term 'race' cements a difference high enough in the Linnaean system such that the charge of cannibalism should no longer apply. Admittedly, there was some precedent in the period for thinking of meat eating in general as a kind of cannibalism. As Michael Parish Lee notes, the 'increased emphasis by the 1870s on the welfare of animals' within the burgeoning movement of vegetarianism 'mark[ed] a growing concern about the cannibalistic implications of meat eating after the popularization of evolutionary theory'. 'Victorian culture',

---

[116] Wells, *Time Machine*, pp. 116, 125.   [117] Hurley, *Gothic Body*, p. 86.

[118] Wells, *Time Machine*, p. 125.

[119] Kathryn Hume, 'Eat or be Eaten: H. G. Wells's *Time Machine*', *Philological Quarterly* 69:2 (Spring 1990): pp. 233–251 (p. 244).

[120] Wells, *Time Machine*, p. 107.

Lee elaborates, 'faced the idea that the line between humans and animals might not be one of division but of lineage. For many, this idea triggered the possibility that those animals consumed as meat were not essentially different from the "we" who ate them'. Regarding *The Time Machine*, we are again confronted with a disparity between the symbolic and the diegetic. Lee is absolutely right, after all, to state that 'the very ambiguity of the underground meat hints, through association, at an underlying [cannibalistic] ambiguity of meat in general'.[121] But if the Traveller was accusing the Morlocks of this far-reaching form of cannibalism, it is unlikely that he himself would, upon his return from the future, ask his house guests as he does to '[s]ave [him] some of that mutton', 'starving' as he was 'for a bit of meat'.[122] Anticipating the argument of the next section, already we can see that the Traveller's sympathy with the Eloi *qua* livestock is not an uncomplicated one; regardless, the Traveller's charge of cannibalism is more symbolic than it is diegetic, adding to the Morlocks' carnivorous nature an abject and horrifying resonance.

But though the Traveller concludes that the 'red joint' he saw upon the table was in fact a meal, a second yet equally predatory possibility haunts his discovery. Let us consider the scene once more, this time in its entirety:

> Presently the walls fell away from me, and I came to a large open space, and, striking another match, saw that I had entered a vast arched cavern, which stretched into utter darkness beyond the range of my light.... Great shapes like big machines rose out of the dimness, and cast grotesque black shadows, in which dim spectral Morlocks sheltered from the glare. The place, by the bye, was very stuffy and oppressive, and the faint halitus of freshly shed blood was in the air. Some way down the central vista was a little table of white metal, laid with what seemed a meal ... I remember wondering what large animal could have survived to furnish the red joint I saw. It was all very indistinct: the heavy smell, the big unmeaning shapes, the obscure figures lurking in the shadows.[123]

The Traveller may have indeed stumbled here upon the Morlocks' dining chamber, but if we take to heart Steven McLean's claim that *The Time Machine* 'invites the reader ... to become actively engaged in the interpretation of the future',[124] then we might as easily deduce that the Traveller has instead stumbled into the laboratory or operating theatre of a Morlock vivisectionist or physiologist. The severed 'red joint' is the centrepiece of a large machinic assemblage, just as physiological laboratories in the latter part of the nineteenth

---

[121] Michael Parish Lee, 'Reading Meat in H. G. Wells', *Studies in the Novel* 42:3 (Fall 2010): 249–268 (pp. 251, 260).

[122] Wells, *Time Machine*, p. 71.   [123] Wells, *Time Machine*, p. 116.

[124] McLean, *Early Fiction*, p. 14.

century were designed for 'the careful incorporation of experimental animals into instrumental mechanisms' such that 'the experimental object increasingly looked like the battery in a machine'. This description comes from Rob Boddice, who also notes that lecture theatres during this time, 'when designed specifically for physiology, tended to be high-banked, semicircular ampitheaters, with the stage set for the physiologist and his apparatus'.[125] The 'arched cavern' evokes the semicircular design of these theatres, and the 'little table of white metal' in the centre certainly seems closer in essence to the operating table than it does to the dinner table. At the very least, the Traveller certainly feels like the object of the medical theatre's gaze: '[t]he sense of these unseen creatures examining me was indescribably unpleasant', he recounts.[126] Rounding out this multi-sensory image is 'the faint halitus of freshly-shed blood', a sensory affront as common to the operating theatre as the butcher's shop. For his part, Wells was well prepared to represent such a space given his earlier experience as a student in Biology at the Normal School of Science.

Diegetic possibilities aside, the metaphorical association of the Morlocks with the stereotype of the callous Victorian vivisectionist haunts the novel beyond the underground chamber and its centrepiece of red meat. Specifically, the Morlocks demonstrate that they share in the vivisectionist's interest in taking things apart for the sake of understanding their mechanism. This fact becomes apparent to the Traveller when he retrieves his stolen machine from the Morlocks. 'I was surprised', the Traveller reports, 'to find it had been carefully oiled and cleaned. I have suspected since that the Morlocks had even partially taken it to pieces while trying in their dim way to grasp its purpose'.[127] The Traveller's disparaging of the Morlock intelligence here is unwarranted; they were not only curious enough to take the machine apart but also possessed enough adaptive ingenuity to put it back together in the correct way such that it worked when the Traveller went to use it again. Just how intelligent, of course, remains unexplored by the text, for even if they were intelligent enough to figure out how to do so, they would not have been able to operate the time machine, since the Traveller had removed and taken with him the levers required for it to work. Regardless, the Morlocks demonstrate a propensity for mechanism that goes beyond rote habit, for they are actively interested in and capable of learning about the construction of unfamiliar objects. Even if we assume for the moment that their interest in mechanism is purely one for non-organic machines, the Morlocks' carnivorousness nonetheless lends metaphorical resonance to their interest in machines. As Lee argues,

[125] Boddice, *Sympathy*, pp. 80, 81.   [126] Wells, *Time Machine*, p. 117.
[127] Wells, *Time Machine*, p. 143.

The Time Machine 'suggest[s] that seeing, knowing, and examining are essentially linked to appetite, that both our scientific observations and our interactions with other people are fundamentally predicated on the desire to consume the subjects we confront'.[128] Lee's astute reading here is premised on the canonical version of the novel, but this metaphorical resonance only becomes more clear when we look not only at the final published version of *The Time Machine* but also at Wells's early drafts and other writings in the years leading up to it.

As is well known, the social and scientific consequences of vivisection were a recurring fixation for Wells. Nowhere is this fixation more obvious than in his follow-up to *The Time Machine*, *The Island of Doctor Moreau*, in which the titular doctor subjects animals to painful experiments so as to create artificial yet humanoid 'Beast Folk'. *Moreau* was not, however, Wells's first foray into commenting on vivisection. In February of 1894 – notably one month before the first version of *The Time Machine* would begin serialisation – Wells published 'The Province of Pain', a short article in which he distinguishes pain from other sensations and other animal reflexes, thus arguing that pain amongst animals might be less common than the average person might think. Tellingly, Wells opens the article with an implicit criticism of 'the activity of the Society for the Prevention of Cruelty to Animals … [and] the zealous enemies of the British Institute of Preventive Medicine', thus setting his argument against the anti-vivisectionists of the day and their appeals to animal pain for the sake of their own arguments.[129] Wells would even go on to recycle some of the arguments in this article to compose Moreau's stated justifications for his horrifying experiments, a fact that both confirms Wells's early fixation on issues regarding vivisection that would recur in later work and at the same time complicates any consistent notion we might have on Wells's views on the topic at the time, for if the titular character of *Moreau* is meant to be the villain, why justify his crimes with one's own beliefs?[130] Regardless, the timing of the publication of 'The Province of Pain' is notable, for it demonstrates that vivisection was not a topic to which Wells turned only after completing *The Time Machine*.

Over the following few years, Wells would publish multiple drafts of *The Time Machine* leading up to the final version. In addition to the *National Observer* version serialised between March and June 1894, Wells also serialised

---

[128] Lee, 'Reading Meat', p. 252.

[129] In H. G. Wells, *The Island of Doctor Moreau*, edited by Mason Harris (Peterborough: Broadview Press, 2009), p. 270. 'The Province of Pain' appears in its entirety in an appendix, pp. 270–274.

[130] By 1928, Wells had settled on whole-heartedly supporting vivisection and defended the practice in an article entitled 'Popular Feeling and the Advancement of Science. Anti-Vivisection'. Like 'The Province of Pain', this article is also included in its entirety in Wells, *Moreau*, pp. 266–269.

a second draft of the novel in the *New Review* between January and June of 1895; the publication of the 'final' version in book form overlapped with the latter serialisation, appearing in May of 1895. Each of the two earlier versions includes a scene, absent from the final version, that reveals Wells had vivisection on the mind while working on the novel. In the first version, the Traveller considers explicitly the possibility that the Morlocks' might be interested not only in artificial mechanisms but also in those of the biological: 'I think they were far more powerfully attracted by the Time Machine than by myself. Their minds were essentially mechanical. That, indeed, was one of the dismal thoughts that came to me – that possibly they would try to take me to pieces and investigate my construction'.[131] The shift in focus here is indicative of the increasing encroachment of scientific inquiry into the animal body. While the Traveller at first consoles himself with the thought the Morlocks would only be interested in the construction of the machine, this thought is immediately undermined by the notion that his own body is merely another form of mechanism under the physiological gaze.

In the second serialised draft, Wells removed this bit of dialogue, but he also added a scene that implicates the Traveller, and by extension the Morlocks, in the same sort of callous interest in procuring and classifying specimens. Jumping ahead many years beyond that of 802 701, the Traveller discovers a group of small creatures akin to 'rabbits, or some small breed of kangaroo'. Interested in 'perhaps secur[ing] a specimen', the Traveller kills one with a rock; he then determines from the shape of its feet and head that the creature is likely an evolutionary descendant of humanity, though a giant centipede takes his kill from him before he can 'examine its teeth and other anatomical points which might show human characteristics'. Despite this discovery of potential human ancestry and the 'disagreeable apprehension' that accompanies it, the Traveller persists in trying to secure another specimen, 'ma[king] several attempts to kill or capture another of the greyish vermin'.[132] In this scene, the roles are of course reversed, with the Traveller now in the position of causing harm to a Morlock-esque grey animal for the sake of learning about it. But in the same way that the Traveller's meal of mutton upon his return to the present stands in stark agreement with the carnivorousness of the Morlocks, so too does this scene reflect that of the grey creatures' callous interest in studying and categorising an object's component parts, whether that object is artificial or biological. In other words, if the Morlocks are meant to figure the defamiliarised human being, then the actions of the sole human being in the narrative are likely

---

[131] Philmus and Hughes (eds.), *Early Writings*, p. 87.
[132] Philmus and Hughes (eds.), *Early Writings*, pp. 97, 99.

to resonate with those of the Morlocks, and thus both the carnivorousness and the callous inquisitiveness of the Traveller can be attributed to the Morlocks by extension. Again, Wells would remove this scene from the next, and what would be final, draft of the novel. It is a peculiar choice – if he wished to remove the obvious hypocrisy in the Traveller's killing of the rabbit-kangaroo, then one wonders why Wells retained the equally obvious hypocrisy of the Traveller's desire for meat upon his return to the present. Regardless, though it is not as glaring as the supposedly bestial hunger of animal predation, the callous inquisitiveness of the Victorian vivisectionist undoubtedly haunts the figure of the Morlocks; by extension, the Eloi are thus at once figured as livestock and experimental specimen.

3.3 'A Vicious Sympathy with Some of Their Ways'

By sympathising with the Eloi, the Traveller at once models both the vegetarian's sympathy for the livestock that humans consume and the antivivisectionist's sympathy for the animal specimen on the operating table. Vegetarianism and anti-vivisection had both been increasingly prevalent in England over the half century preceding the publication of *The Time Machine*,[133] and the nature of the Eloi's sympathetic appeals would not have been entirely out of place in either discourse. When the Traveller states that 'the Eloi had kept too much of their human form not to claim my sympathy, and to make me perforce a sharer in their degradation and their Fear', it is the hypothetical fear of both the domesticated cow and the vivisected dog that the Traveller is temporarily capable of imagining; that it takes the 'human form' to assist the Traveller in imagining such a fate does not detract fully from the radical traversal of difference such sympathies facilitate. And yet, we have seen how fickle these sympathies ultimately are. Neither the Traveller's sympathy for livestock nor his sympathy for animal specimens travels with him when he leaves the year 802 701, for he feels no qualms towards eating his dinner of mutton or bashing in the skull of the naive posthuman rabbit-kangaroo. We might be tempted, of course, to read the Traveller's hypocrisies as themselves carrying didactic weight, as if Wells wishes for us to judge the Traveller's actions accordingly. Yet, Wells was by no means a supporter of vegetarianism or anti-vivisection. We have seen that the latter was the case in his consideration of the subject in 'The Province of Pain'; as for the former, Wells's depictions of the frugivorous Eloi makes it difficult to read *The Time Machine* as wholeheartedly supporting a meatless diet.

---

[133] See Emelia Quinn, *Reading Veganism: The Monstrous Vegan, 1818 to Present* (Oxford: Oxford University Press, 2021), pp. 63–66. Oddly, Quinn notes that 'despite their seeming natural affinity, there was often little relationship between anti-vivisection and vegetarianism', p. 65.

As Emelia Quinn rightly notes in her monograph on the figure of the 'Monstrous Vegan', 'the Eloi's veganism is presented as a mode of degeneration in which humanity no longer stands distinct from the animal kingdom, having lost their ability for language and reason'.[134] Similarly, Colton Valentine observes that the pre-storytelling dinner of 'meat propels the Traveller though 60-odd pages of reportage, whereas fruit barely moves the Eloi to utter a few definitional words'.[135] Just as the supporter of vivisection and experimental physiology would argue that the 'a small amount of suffering ought to be permitted if it eliminates a larger amount of suffering by its results',[136] so too does Wells seem to imply in *The Time Machine* that at least some amount of meat eating is necessary for the species to stave off mental and physical decline.

For Wells, it seems, sympathy for animals does not (or perhaps should not) motivate a change in one's behaviour towards the natural world. This stance towards sympathy is in fact recognisable in all of Wells's most famous early novels. *The Island of Doctor Moreau*, perhaps Wells's most explicit exploration of the potential for human sympathy with non-human animals and their suffering, is starkly ambivalent about the consequences of such an exploration. The novel's narrator, Prendick, notably responds empathically to the cry of a puma, as Moreau subjects the creature to a painful process of vivisection in the name of transforming it into one of his humanoid 'Beast Folk'. 'The emotional appeal of those yells grew upon me steadily', Prendick notes, until it felt 'as if all the pain in the world had found a voice'. Taking a Humean approach to the phenomenon, Prendick then observes, '[i]t is when suffering finds a voice and sets our nerves quivering that this pity comes troubling us'.[137] While Sherryl Vint argues that '[t]he empathy Prendick felt for the puma woman suggests [a model] consistent with the feminist embrace of the other', Andrew Bishop notes that Prendick also 'redefine[s] sympathy as a nervous reflex, a "lower" animal impulse better off suppressed or cured rather than heeded'.[138] The ethical status of cross-species sympathy is thus deeply ambiguous in *Moreau*, and nowhere is this ambiguity more apparent than in the juxtaposition between Moreau and his assistant, Montgomery. On the one hand, Moreau's frank disregard for '[s]ympathetic pain' – 'all I know of it', he notes, 'I remember as a thing I used to suffer from years ago' – is clearly meant to stand in horrifying juxtaposition to

[134] Quinn, *Reading Veganism*, p. 87.

[135] Colton Valentine, 'H. G. Wells and the Fin-de-Siècle Gustatory Paradox', *The Review of English Studies* 71:302 (2020): 937–951 (p. 944).

[136] Boddice, *Sympathy*, p. 95.   [137] Wells, *Moreau*, p. 97.

[138] Sherryl Vint, 'Animals and Animality from the Island of Moreau to the Uplift Universe', *The Yearbook of English Studies* 37:2 (2007): 85–102 (p. 94); Andrew Bishop, 'Making Sympathy "Vicious" on *The Island of Dr. Moreau*', *Nineteenth-Century Contexts* 43:2 (2021): 205–220 (p. 206).

Montgomery's 'ill-concealed irritation at the noise of the vivisected puma'. Prendick, after all, notes that though he 'distrusted and dreaded Moreau', Montgomery 'was a man [he] felt [he] understood'. On the other hand, Prendick also evinces an implicit judgement on Montgomery and his 'sneaking kindness with some of these metamorphosed brutes, [his] vicious sympathy with some of their ways'.[139] Just what makes this sympathy 'vicious' and 'sneaking' is not made clear by Wells, especially given the Beast Folk are predominantly peaceful and vegetarian; that is, until Montgomery shares his liquor with the Beast Men, a choice that leads to a drunken brawl and ends in Montgomery's death. The novel thus sets up an irresolvable disjunction between Moreau's callousness and Montgomery's 'vicious sympathy', neither of which the novel seems to support in any sort of didactic sense.

Compared to *Moreau*, Wells's *The War of the Worlds* seems at first glance to offer a reasonably straightforward exploration into the potential for cross-species sympathy, but even here Wells refuses to leave off on an unambiguous note. Characters in the novel repeatedly compare their own suffering under the Martian occupation to the experience of animals suffering the same from humans, and over the course of only a couple chapters these comparisons move increasingly further from the typically 'human' sphere of compassion. The novel's narrator first notes that he 'touched an emotion beyond the common range of men' as he 'felt as a rabbit might feel returning to his burrow and suddenly confronted by the work of a dozen busy navvies [i.e "manual labourers"] digging the foundations of a house'.[140] Being cute and cuddly, a rabbit is a reasonably easy animal with whom one might sympathise, but not so for the narrator's next object of sympathetic consideration: 'I ... crept out of the house like a rat leaving its hiding place – a creature scarcely larger, an inferior animal, a thing that for any passing whim of our masters might be hunted and killed'. The narrator then includes an explicitly compassionate reflection on this imaginative identification, stating, '[s]urely, if we have learned nothing else, this war has taught us pity – pity for those witless souls that suffer our domination'. Stretching this sympathetic identification even further beyond the mammalian realm, a lone and despondent artillery-man remarks to the narrator, 'ants build their cities, live their lives, have wars, revolutions, until the men want them out of the way, and then they go out of the way. That's what we are now – just ants'.[141] In each of these three cases, a human being finds themself capable of enacting a Smithean imaginative

---

[139] Wells, *Moreau*, pp. 127, 96, 121, 135.

[140] H. G. Wells, *The War of the Worlds*, edited by Martin A. Danahay (Peterborough: Broadview Press, 2003), p. 160. Definition of 'navvies' provided by Danahay's footnotes.

[141] Wells, *War of the Worlds*, pp. 164, 167.

transport into the experience of a distinctly non-human Other, a sympathetic transport that in at least one instance leads to an explicit feeling of pity for an animal that normally incites fear and disgust. For Christina Alt, these and other examples demonstrate that '*The War of the Worlds* is thus underpinned by an idealization of sympathy', and consequently the novel's 'evolutionary pessimism is tempered by the emergence of a new experience of empathy across species boundaries'.[142] While Alt's reading is astute, Wells's narrator ends his story nonetheless with a comment that suggests his time under Martian domination has not soured him entirely to the thought of human domination of other species. 'When the slow cooling of the sun makes earth uninhabitable', the narrator muses only a few paragraphs from the end, 'it may be that the thread of life that has begun here will have streamed out and caught our sister planet [i.e. Mars] within its toils. Should we conquer?' To this question, the narrator answers with an implicit yes, for 'wonderful' is the thought he has of humankind colonising other planets.[143] Clearly, the pity he felt 'for those witless souls that suffer our domination' did not lead the narrator to renounce domination as such, for he retains an enthusiasm for colonial conquest and the subjugation of non-human beings.

Far from unique in its tendency to befuddle, *The Time Machine* shares with *Moreau* and *War of the Worlds* an ambiguous view toward the value of cross-species sympathy. In all three, Wells sets up sympathetic relationships with non-human animals who are suffering or threatened, but these relationships do not or perhaps cannot incite a change of behaviour or bring relief to the suffering creature. Wells tended to see nature as a zero-sum game in which domination of one species over another was inevitable.[144] To what end, then, does Wells spend so much time imagining, writing and allegorising the suffering of animals? What might explain the relish with which Wells engages in these sympathetic excursions into animal suffering? One can only speculate, of course, but we may get a hint from a passage of the aforementioned essay, 'The Province of Pain':

> No scientific observer has, as yet, crept into the animal mind . . . We can only reason that there is evidence of pain from analogy, a method of proof too apt to display a wayward fancy to be a sure guide. This alone, however, does not

---

[142] Christina Alt, 'Extinction, Extermination, and the Ecological Optimism of H. G. Wells', in Gerry Canavan and Kim Stanley Robinson (eds.), *Green Planets: Ecology and Science Fiction* (Middletown: Wesleyan University Press, 2014), pp. 25–39 (pp. 29, 30).

[143] Wells, *War of the Worlds*, p. 190.

[144] This worldview is apparent in many of Wells's early science articles, such as 'On Extinction' and 'The Extinction of Man'. For the former, see Philmus and Hughes (eds.), *Early Writings*, pp. 169–172; for the latter, see H. G. Wells, *Certain Personal Matters*, pp. 115–119. www.gutenberg.org/files/17508/17508-h/17508-h.htm [last accessed 1 September 2023].

prevent us discussing the question – rather the reverse, for there is, at least, the charm of uncertainty about any inquiries how animals feel pain. It is speculation almost at its purest.[145]

Wells is, of course, one of the early trailblazers of employing fiction for 'speculation at its purest'. Might his literary forays into cross-species sympathy be an attempt to achieve the impossible, to 'cre[ep] into the animal mind'? If so, Wells's speculative sympathy would appear to be a psychological version of the same interest that drives the vivisectionist to cut up the animal to know it inside and out. Here, the speculative author appears to strive both to know and to subsume the Other so thoroughly that they can come to understand even their most intimate suffering as well. Such sympathy would be the voyeuristic urge to know vicariously what one wishes not to experience concretely, a masochistic hijacking of the sympathetic faculties and a sympathy far more vicious than anything on the island of Moreau.

4 Matheson's Dialectic of Posthuman Sympathy

Richard Matheson's *I Am Legend* is in many respects a hybrid of both *The Last Man* and *The Time Machine*. Like the former, the world of Matheson's novel is afflicted by an airborne plague, against which the novel's main character attempts to fortify the walls of his house in an inversion of the plague-ridden Constantinople; like the latter, Matheson's Last Man faces a threat from a predatory nocturnal being, one that shares in the Morlocks' affinity with animals often deemed 'pests' and 'vermin'. Like those of *The Last Man* and *The Time Machine*, the plot of *I Am Legend* is as much shaped and constrained by demarcations, boundaries and borders as it is characterised by the transgres-
sion of such borders. The story is set in Los Angeles some months after the outbreak of a global pandemic of vampirism. Spreading partially via contagious insect, bat and vampire bites and partially via sporulated bacteria blown about in dust clouds, the *vampiris* germ succeeds in transforming most of the world's population into vampires. While many of these vampires were once living humans who died of the plague and returned as true 'undead', many others are still technically 'alive' but are nonetheless infected: they also crave human blood, have an adverse reaction to garlic, and can only come out at night. Robert Neville, who believes himself to be the last uninfected human being, spends his days alternating between fortifying his house and searching shadowed places for vampires to slay; his nights, by contrast, are spent hiding within his house while vampires congregate outside and attempt to break in. Neville's solitary life is thus strictly regulated both temporally and spatially by literal borders: the

---

[145] In Wells, *Moreau*, p. 270.

former as the divide between day and night; the latter not only as the walls between him and the besieging vampires but also the maximum distance he can travel by day before needing to stop and return home before nightfall. One could also add as a literal border Neville's immune system, which divides the infected outside world from his own blood's natural immunity to the vampire plague.

Many commentators have noted how these literal boundaries support and metaphorise Neville's attempts to preserve the conceptual boundaries intrinsic to binary modes of thinking. Rhonda Knight notes Neville's attachment to 'majoritarian thinking which indicates that humans are the world's most dominant species', and guided by such thinking, Neville 'struggle[s] to maintain his literal and metaphorical boundaries in order to remain human in a world without humans'.[146] Simchi Cohen lists many such conceptual boundaries that Neville works to uphold, claiming that *I Am Legend* is a 'narrative saturated in the fear of contagion, in the strict demarcations between human and inhuman, diseased and healthy, normal and abnormal'.[147] Similarly, Chris Koenig-Woodyard rightly states, 'Matheson's portrait of Neville is characterized by an intense and increasing resistance to the inhuman, his humanity standing in binary opposition to the vampiric'.[148] In sum, it is the very existence of the vampire on the other side of his front door that gives Neville a monster against which to define and to defend his own humanity, an Other against which to define and to defend his very Self. It almost goes without saying that these binaries are not neutral or equally weighted from Neville's perspective, for Matheson's Last Man sees himself as the standard of normalcy against which the vampire is an aberration, thus justifying his wholesale slaughter of the dormant vampires during the day. As is widely recognised, of course, Neville is able nonetheless to maintain neither fixed boundaries nor fixed binaries as the narrative unfolds. This inability he recognises far too late, for it is only after he has been captured and is awaiting execution at the hands of a new society of living vampires that he comes to recognise that '[n]ormalcy was a majority concept, the standard of many and not the standard of just one man'.[149] This recognition accompanies the most significant binary breakdown in the text, what Koenig-Woodyard calls 'Matheson's monstrification of Neville'[150] – Neville's discovery that he has in

---

[146] Rhonda Knight, 'Evolving the Human in Richard Matheson's *I Am Legend* and M. R. Carey's Hungry Plague Novels', *Supernatural Studies: An Interdisciplinary Journal of Art, Media, and Culture* 7:1 (2021): 50–72 (pp. 55, 56).

[147] Simchi Cohen, 'The Legend of Disorder: The Living Dead, Disorder and Autoimmunity in Richard Matheson's *I Am Legend*', *Horror Studies* 5:1 (2014): 47–63 (p. 48).

[148] Chris Koenig-Woodyard, '"Lovie – is the vampire so bad?": Posthuman Rhetoric in Richard Matheson's *I Am Legend*', in Anya Heise-von der Lippe (ed.), *Posthuman Gothic* (Cardiff: University of Wales Press, 2017), pp. 77–92 (p. 83).

[149] Richard Matheson, *I Am Legend* (New York: Tom Doherty Associates, 1995), p. 169.

[150] Koenig-Woodyard, 'The Mathematics of Monstrosity', p. 85.

fact become the legendary fear-inducing, Dracula-esque monster in the eyes of this new vampire society.

Neville's inability to maintain the various binaries that structure his view of himself, of his world and of his normative superiority is unsurprising given that the monster, to again quote Jeffery Jerome Cohen, 'refuses easy categorization . . . [a]nd so the monster is dangerous, a form suspended between forms that threaten to smash distinctions'.[151] The very first line of *I Am Legend*, in fact, foreshadows the text's propensity to undermine and complicate all binaries throughout: 'On those cloudy days, Robert Neville was never sure when sunset came, and sometimes they were in the streets before he could get back'. The delineation between the day-realm of humanity and the night-realm of the vampire is revealed from the outset to be unreliable, obfuscatable and transgressible, and thus the text's gradual breakdown of binary distinctions is both figuratively and literally fore-*shadowed* by the cloud's blocking of the sun. Similarly, while Neville can board up his home against the vampire threat, the method of contagion of the vampire virus is first suspected and then ultimately revealed to travel not only via contagious bite but also in a diffuse form through the air via the dust storms that had become commonplace in the aftermath of a nuclear war. In an early flashback, the text showcases the dust's tenacious ability to bypass all methods of quarantine and containment:

> There had been another dust storm during the night. High, spinning winds had scoured the house with grit, driven it through the cracks, sifted it through the plaster pores, and left a hair-thin layer of dust across the furniture surfaces. Over their bed the dust filtered like fine powder, settling in their hair and on their eyelids and under their nails, clogging their pores.

Later, as Neville seeks to determine the cause of the vampire contagion, his germ hypothesis leads him to suspect that the dust storms might have permitted a sporulated version of the virus to spread: 'The freed spores would be blown about by the storms. They could lodge in minute skin abrasions caused by the scaling dust. Once in the skin, the spore could germinate and multiply by fission'.[152] By the end, Neville's theories regarding the dust storms are proven correct, and thus like the obscuring clouds that muddle the divide between day and night, the vampire germ's ease at transgressing boundaries models the breakdown of binary divisions that characterise Neville's story.

Sympathy too, as we have seen, is a transgressor of boundaries, an emotional and affective bridge between Self and Other. Such a transgressive power is one of the central drivers of *I Am Legend*'s plot. Over the course of the novel, Neville is depicted fostering a sympathetic relationship with a dog, struggling to

---

[151] Cohen, 'Monster Theses', p. 45.   [152] Matheson, *I Am Legend*, pp. 13, 51, 88.

sympathise with a seemingly uninfected (yet in fact vampiric) woman, and ultimately sympathising with the very vampires that wish his destruction. This succession of sympathetic endeavours constitute a dialectic of increasingly Other-oriented sympathy, one that ends with the complete sympathetic reversal of Neville *qua* human and vampire *qua* monster, an example of that 'complete sympathy' that is the 'interplay and interchange of places, positions, persons, sentiments and points of view'.[153] Yet *I Am Legend* is a truly dialectical Gordian knot, for at the close of the narrative all has changed yet all remains the same. Dramatising what I call the 'short-circuit dialectic' that is Horkheimer and Adorno's *Dialectic of Enlightenment*, Matheson's living vampires work to eradicate both the remaining uninfected humans and the bestial undead vampires, thus modelling the violent process in which enlightenment thinking comes to 'dominate wholly both [nature] and human beings'.[154] But by sympathising with these undead vampires suffering under the violence of the new vampire society, Neville provides us with a glimpse, however brief, of a posthuman sympathy that thoroughly destabilises the ontological divide between the 'human' and the 'inhuman'.

4.1 'Full Circle. A New Terror'

At once a cause and consequence of Neville's binary thinking is the desire to discover beings with whom Neville can identify and sympathise. Perhaps surprisingly for the supposed last human on earth, Neville finds opportunities over the course of his narrative to try to foster such connections, and the succession of these various opportunities makes up the steps of the novel's dialectic of increasingly Other-oriented sympathy. His first consideration is the most obviously undesirable, representing something akin to the suicidal urge that drove Lord Raymond into Constantinople. Early in the text, Neville goes so far as to consider giving up and joining the vampires that congregate outside his house every night, telling himself that '[i]t was a sure way to be free of them. Be one of them'. Admittedly, Neville does not address how such a transformation could be effected given his blood's natural immunity to the vampire plague, but the desire expressed here is significant nonetheless, as it demonstrates such a profound lack of sympathetic community that he would consider monstrous company over desperate solitude. Yet Neville resists this pseudo-suicidal urge, and not without good reason. While spying through his peephole at the first few vampires to show up on his lawn one particular night, Neville notes the

---

[153] David Marshall quoted in Lamb, *Evolution of Sympathy*, p. 68.

[154] Max Horkheimer and Theodor W. Adorno, *The Dialectic of Enlightenment*, trans. Edmund Jephcott, edited by Gunzelin Schmid Noeri (Stanford: Stanford University Press, 2002), p. 2.

atomistic nature of the undead's behaviour: 'None of the three was speaking to either of the others. They never did. They walked and walked about on restless feet, circling each other like wolves, never looking at each other once, having hungry eyes only for the house and their prey inside the house'.[155] The choice to become one with the vampires would thus be nothing more than the choice to become permanently 'one' – singular, atomised – amongst other vampires. Neville's conceptually binary and manifestly enforced separation between himself and the vampires is not one of entirely undeserved prejudice, for Neville can see with his own eyes that these creatures, like the Eloi of Wells's future London, demonstrate nothing of the sympathetic connection that he seeks. Neville thus enacts a profound paradox: he fiercely guards his atomistic individuality for the sake of staving off atomistic individuality.

The next turn of the dialectic sees Neville move from confronting unsympathetic (in)difference to cultivating sympathetic recognition. Like Shelley's Verney, Neville *qua* Last Man fosters sympathy most successfully with a dog; also like Verney, Neville finds the dog to be closer to the realm of human affairs than the realm of nature, here represented by the pestiferous vampires. Tellingly, the discovery of the dog saves Neville from a particularly pessimistic period in which he tries to drink both his problems and his humanity away: 'I'm an animal', he exclaims, 'I'm a *dumb, stupid* animal and I'm going to drink!' Simply put, the dog brings Neville from the brink of 'animality' back to 'humanity'. Over the course of this venture, Neville extends to the dog many of the different kinds of sympathy that we have seen over the course of this *Element*. Neville first employs a Smithean imaginative transport for the sake of helping him understand the dog's experience:

> He forced himself to think of what the dog must have gone through. The endless nights of groveling in the blackness, hidden God knows where, its gaunt chest laboring in the night while all around its shivering form the vampires walked. The foraging for food and water, the struggle for life in a world without masters, housed in a body that man had made dependent on himself.

At this point in the story, the dog has yet to learn to trust Neville and thus flees from the man, frustrating him greatly. However, while Neville must at first push through his frustration and 'forc[e] himself' to sympathise with the dog, the exercise ultimately brings him to a mood of compassion, pity, and goodwill, for afterwards he thinks, '[p]oor little fella . . . I'll be good to you when you come to live with me'. This compassionate disposition toward the dog helps to further their relationship, until Neville comes to recognise the dog's own receptive

---

[155] Matheson, *I Am Legend*, pp. 29, 65.

recognition of his voice and sees in the dog's eyes a consciousness with whom he can understand and sympathise:

> A sudden smile of delight raised his lips as he saw the dog's good ear stand up. He's listening! he thought excitedly. He hears what I say, the little son of a gun! … The dog looked at him curiously, its good ear twitching again. Those eyes, Neville thought. What a world of feeling in those eyes! Distrust, fear, hope, loneliness – all etched in those big brown eyes.

This moment of sympathetic recognition is much like that which Walton desired at the outset of *Frankenstein*: Neville can see the dog seeing him, can recognise the dog's recognition of his own being. In time, the dog even begins speaking back to Neville, 'barking its curt acknowledgment' after its meal.[156]

If an author is to the character as the Creator is to the creation, then Matheson is a fickle and vindictive god. In this unfolding dialectic between Self and Other, Neville will be tested twice: first, by the tragic death of the dog; second, by the appearance of a purportedly uninfected yet in fact mal-evolently vampiric woman named Ruth. Neville's fortitude will be tested in both instances, though not in the same way. Much as the intimate sympathies between Perdita and Raymond led the former to feel her own existential obliteration upon the death of the latter, so too does the tragic death of the dog trigger a profound change in Neville. Despite his best efforts, the dog becomes infected by the vampire plague before Neville can foster a fully trusting companionship with the animal. A brief, yet heart-rending, glimpse of what could have been between these two beings marks the tragic aporia in Neville's pursuit of sympathy:

> The dog looked up at him with its dulled, sick eyes and then its tongue faltered out and licked roughly and moistly across the palm of Neville's hand.
> Something broke in Neville's throat. He sat there silently while tears ran slowly down his cheeks.
> In a week the dog was dead.

This 'something' that breaks in Neville is any hope he may have had of someday finding a lasting sympathetic connection with another being. While he does not go to the same suicidal lengths as Perdita, he does commit a kind of emotional suicide, closing himself off completely by 'learn[ing] to accept the dungeon he existed in'.[157] The barricaded door of his house thus comes to figure his own psychological state, for just as he closes off the entry to his home, so too does he close off the entry to his heart.

[156] Matheson, *I Am Legend*, pp. 92, 100, 103, 104.   [157] Matheson, *I Am Legend*, pp. 110, 111.

The death of the dog tests the fortitude of Neville's will and his drive to continue living; the appearance of Ruth will test the fortitude of the emotional walls he has since erected. Following the death of the dog and the profound solitude he accepts as a result, Neville finds he does not wish to connect with Ruth given the emotional defences he has erected. 'He was afraid', Matheson writes, 'of giving out his heart, of removing the chains he had forged around it to keep emotion prisoner'. This expression of fear follows the thought of him and Ruth 'establish[ing] a relationship, perhaps becom[ing] husband and wife, hav[ing] children', a thought that for Neville is 'more terrifying' than the thought of Ruth being potentially infected. In response to what he interprets as a flirtatious movement by Ruth, Neville finds himself 'irritated' as opposed to 'attracted', and we the audience are then given a glimpse of his stubbornly closed-off internal state told in free indirect style: '[a]s the moments passed he could almost sense himself drifting farther and farther from her. In a way he almost regretted having found her at all. Through the years he had achieved a certain degree of peace. He had accepted solitude, found it not half bad. Now this ... ending it all'.[158] In his enforcement of the boundary between the safety of his house and the threat of the vampire world – allegorically a preservation of the divide between his Self and the threat of the Other – Neville comes to embody the very atomised lifestyle he so despises in the vampires. Without sympathetic connection, he has become the very thing he hoped to avoid, yet it was also the failure of his pursuit for sympathy with the dog that most fully pushed him into an acceptance of this atomised lifestyle. As it was for Shelley's Verney, sympathy is both a potential solution to and a potential cause of lonesome despair.

But Neville's defences do not hold, and his opening up to Ruth incites the dialectic of Self and Other to turn again. After sharing a moment of togetherness 'sitting in the darkness, pressing close together, as if all the heat in the world were in their bodies and they would share the warmth between them', Neville comes to learn that this woman with whom he has made himself vulnerable is in fact a vampire sent to spy on him. Ruth is a member of a new community of living vampires who have discovered a medication to manage the *vampiris* bacteria in their blood, converting what was a parasitically fatal relationship between germ and host into a symbiotic one. The living vampires have thus discovered a way to pacify the vampire Other living in their own bodies; conversely, Neville, having rendered himself vulnerable to the Other whom he has invited in, has found betrayal as the only reward for his sympathies, for the new vampire society intends on wiping out the one whom they see as 'the last of the old race'.[159] Going into the final scenes of the novel, then, both Neville and the audience are

---

[158] Matheson, *I Am Legend*, pp. 139, 141.   [159] Matheson, *I Am Legend*, pp. 150, 167.

left with an uncomfortable aporia: embrace the safety of atomistic individuality and become the Other, or open yourself up and leave oneself vulnerable to the Other. Either way, the Other enters, the vampire is invited to cross the threshold – a fatal invitation, to which the old vampire mythologies attest. *I Am Legend* thus evinces many of the same prejudicial anxieties toward the Other that are evoked by early examples of the vampire legend, such as fears of racial miscegenation, xenophobic suspicions toward immigrants and foreigners, and aversions to the infected blood of (often queer-coded) 'degenerates'. As it was in *The Last Man*'s depiction of the plague-ridden Constantinople *qua* orientalised and infectious Other, these vampire legends suggest that opening up to such Others through sympathy renders one extremely vulnerable; by playing into these tropes, *I Am Legend* should leave us feely rightly uncomfortable.[160]

And yet, *I Am Legend* doesn't remain at this dialectical level either, for its closing scenes provide new opportunities for sympathy with the vampire and thus with the Other in general by metaphorical extension. Since Neville would slay both the living and the undead vampires he came across, the members of the new vampire community – the one composed of living vampires to which Ruth belongs – regards Neville neither as human nor as humane but instead as the murderous and aberrant monster against which their new identity is to be formed and from which their new society must be protected. The full gravity of this final Gothic inversion hits Neville in the closing lines of the novel, as he awaits execution before a crowd of these living vampires:

> Robert Neville looked out over the new people of the earth. He knew he did not belong to them; he knew that, like the [undead] vampires, he was anathema and black terror to be destroyed. And, abruptly, the concept came, amusing to him even in his pain.... Full circle, he thought.... Full circle. A new terror born in death, a new superstition entering the unassailable fortress of forever. I am legend.[161]

What thus begins with a literal crossing of a boundary, namely the vampire Ruth's entering of Neville's fortress-like house, ends with a crossing of the conceptual boundary between Neville *qua* normative superiority and the Vampire *qua* aberrant monster. This transformation is the apex of 'Matheson's monstrification of Neville', to again quote Koenig-Woodyard,[162] and notably

[160] For an insightful reading of *I Am Legend* in the context of colonial America and early zombie films, which thus distinguishes the novel from the colonial anxieties of European Vampire stories, see Adryan Glasgow, '"Wild Work": The Monstrosity of Whiteness in *I Am Legend*', in Cheyenne Mathews and Janet V. Haedicke (eds.), *Reading Richard Matheson: A Critical Survey* (Lanham, Maryland: Rowman & Littlefield, 2014), pp. 31–43.
[161] Matheson, *I Am Legend*, p. 170.
[162] Koenig-Woodyard, 'The Mathematics of Monstrosity', 85.

this monstrification is itself a form of sympathetic inversion. Looking out of his cell window, Neville sees on the faces of the congregated vampires a mix of 'awe, fear [and] shrinking horror', and with this 'he understood what they felt and did not hate them'.[163] This moment of understanding is a sympathy in many respects far more profound than that with the dog, for here Neville is not sympathising with a being that engages in a mutually sympathetic recognition but with a being that resists sympathy for him, that sees him as a monster and thus refuses any recognition on their part. Neville's journey from Last Man to monstrous legend thus proceeds by way of a dialectic of sympathy across a wide range of relations between Self and Other: from the initial confrontation with unsympathetic (in)difference, through stages of sympathetic recognition, a-sympathetic self-defence and betrayed vulnerability, and ultimately to an experience of Gothic sympathy that succeeds in transforming the sympathiser into the very monster against whom he believed he was defending himself.

4.2 'He Felt More Deeply toward the [Undead] Vampires'

At first glance, the aforementioned seems like a rather straightforward dialectic a la the beginning of chapter four of Hegel's *Phenomenology of Spirit*, the infamous dialectical staging that sees the Self's desire for the Other transform into desire for the recognition of the Self by the Other, which in turn becomes a hierarchised domination of the Lord over the Bondsman that lays the very conditions out of which the Bondsman will topple the domination of the Lord. Neville at first desires the company of another – any other, 'a man, a woman, a child, it didn't matter'[164] – and temporarily finds sympathy in the mutual recognition of the dog; the loss of recognition with the dog's death sets the stage for Neville's implicit confrontation with Ruth and ultimately the explicit confrontation with the entirety of the vampire society, a confrontation that sees the former hierarchy toppled and the two poles of normative superiority and aberrant submission inverted. For Koenig-Woodyard, something akin to what I have described here enacts in the novel what he calls a 'dialectics of the posthuman: the novella is structured with and around pairs, doubles, dualities and oppositions – binaries that abrade internally, potentially expanding to a dialectic that ultimately yields a new third ontological space between the two poles'. Importantly then, for Koenig-Woodyard, the collapse of human/ inhuman binary is not a simple reversal of terms, for what Neville originally believes to be a binary – human contra inhuman – undergoes 'ontological multiplicity' and takes on a tripartite schema: 'the binary of a thesis (human) and an antithesis (the inhuman and vampiric) that potentially synthesize to form

---

[163] Matheson, *I Am Legend*, p. 169.   [164] Matheson, *I Am Legend*, p. 101.

the posthuman'.[165] Just as Hegel's confrontation between the Lord and the Bondsman sees the dialectic movement toward a synthesis that itself becomes but one term for a new dialectical confrontation, so too would the new vampire society *qua* posthuman leave behind the former human/inhuman binary and look forward to new forms and novel dialectical stagings.

There are still knots, however, in Matheson's Gordian weave to untangle. While Koenig-Woodyard's introduction of a third term to complicate the human/inhuman binary is an insightful move, by positing a reconciliation that sees the contradictions of the human/inhuman dichotomy resolved by a higher-order synthesis in the posthuman, this tripartite formulation runs the risk of obfuscating what remains of both the human and the inhuman – namely, the violence of the human/inhuman contradiction – in the emergence of this new vampire society. Indeed, Matheson's society of living vampires retains the same monstrous propensity toward violence, and the same propensity toward rationalising such violence, demonstrated by Neville. Against Neville's scorn, Ruth defends the new society's violent eradication of both the undead vampires and the last remaining non-infected humans by appealing to Neville's own justifications for murdering vampires: 'they are killers – assigned killers, legal killers. They're respected for their killing, admired for it. What can you expect from them? They're only fallible men. And men can learn to enjoy killing. That's an old story, Neville. You know that'. Indeed, by rehearsing this 'old story' of 'repossessing society by violence',[166] the new vampire society does not so much synthesise the human/inhuman contradiction in a higher order as it maintains the contradiction in its very rehearsal of such. For Rhonda Knight, the 'new [vampire] society has already adopted the binarism of majoritarian thinking', for by systematically wiping out the undead vampires, 'the new society shoehorns itself into an outdated paradigm which perpetuates other discourses based on excluding and defeating Otherness'.[167] Similarly, Aspasia Stephanou argues that the new vampire society represents not the radical potential of a posthuman future but a 'new biopolitical order . . . [a] regime of bio-vampire-politics':

> [T]he new race of infected humans shares [Neville's] ideals and certainties. They believe in purity, race, species homogeneity, and life as fundamentally centered on the human. The living vampires or infected humans do not wholly embrace their new condition, instead seeking to correct, manage, and normalize the disease while obsessively extending their lives and banishing death. They do not relish the pollution of boundaries but instead seek to erect new ones.[168]

---

[165] Koenig-Woodyard, 'Posthuman Rhetoric', pp. 83, 79, 88.

[166] Matheson, *I Am Legend*, pp. 167, 166.   [167] Knight, 'Evolving the Human', pp. 57, 59.

[168] Aspasia Stephanou, '"The Last of the Old Race": *I Am Legend* and Bio-Vampire-Politics', in Cheyenne Mathews and Janet V. Haedicke (eds.), *Reading Richard Matheson: A Critical Survey* (Lanham, MD: Rowman & Littlefield, 2014), pp. 17–28 (p. 19).

Thus for Neville to sympathise with these living vampires is only to sympathise with beings that are perpetuating the same violent actions that he once did. To be sure, this is an act of Gothic sympathy, a sympathetic recognition that destabilises identities and monstrifies the sympathiser. Yet the Gothic reversal upon which this sympathy is premised is not in fact that radical of a traversal of difference: the sympathy Neville now feels for the vampire is for members of a society as violent and remorseless as he is, and the binary of human/inhuman is not so much broken down entirely as it is merely inverted.

Neville's dialectical transformation is thus more akin to what I hazard to call the 'short-circuit dialectic' of Horkheimer and Adorno's *The Dialectic of Enlightenment*. In contradistinction to the progressive dialectic of 'thesis-antithesis-synthesis', Horkheimer and Adorno instead posit a dialectical transformation in which binaries are undermined not via higher-order synthesis but rather via the equally Hegelian notion of becoming one's opposite in the very act of distancing oneself from this opposite. Horkheimer and Adorno argue that such a transformation has befallen the enlightenment project, for in its pursuit of 'the disenchantment of the world', enlightenment fell prey to the very same mythological fatalism it was intended to overcome:

> Just as myths already entail enlightenment, with every step enlightenment entangles itself more deeply in mythology. Receiving all its subject matter from myths, in order to destroy them, it falls as judge under the spell of myth. It seeks to escape the trial of fate and retribution by itself exacting retribution on that trial.[169]

What Horkheimer and Adorno describe is an ideological form of Kristeva's abjection, for though enlightenment tries to reject, to denounce and to expel myth, myth stands in relation to enlightenment as that abject 'Other who proceeds and possesses me, and through such possession causes me to be', and thus enlightenment comes to find 'that the impossible constitutes its very *being*, that it is none other than abject'.[170] Importantly, it is enlightenment's domination of nature that undergirds this short-circuit dialectic:

> Myth becomes enlightenment and nature mere objectivity. Human beings purchase the increase in their power with estrangement from that over which it is exerted. Enlightenment stands in the same relationship to things as the dictator to human beings. He knows them to the extent that he can manipulate them. The man of science knows things to the extent that he can make them.

Thus, while it was intended to 'establish man as the master of nature', enlightenment has instead fallen back upon itself to 'dominate wholly both [nature] and

---

[169] Horkheimer and Adorno, *Dialectic*, pp. 1, 8.   [170] Kristeva, *Powers of Horror*, pp. 10, 5.

human beings' – hence the 'triumphant calamity' of two world wars, the nuclear bomb and the Holocaust.[171] Though much of Horkheimer and Adorno's argumentation may not stand to scrutiny today, particularly their own mythologisation of so-called 'primitive' peoples, this formulation of the short-circuit dialectic – the basic schema of enlightenment rationality distancing itself from its opposite only to then become its opposite – is precisely that dialectic dramatised in *I Am Legend*.

Robert Neville begins the novel under the sway of a mythological explanation for the vampire plague, lamenting that 'before science had caught up with the [vampire] legend, the legend had swallowed science'. As the narrative progresses, however, Neville increasingly seeks a scientific explanation for the vampire plague, and so doing he comes to represent the subject of enlightenment rationality in its most obsessive, almost pathological form. He 'won't believe anything unless [he] see[s] it in a microscope', he performs violent and fatal 'experiment[s]' on vampire women, and he 'never once consider[s] the possibility that he might be wrong'.[172] The vampires, for their part, stand against Neville's enlightenment rationality as nature *qua* monster, as a natural world that must be objectified and decoded for the sake of pacification and domination. Their alignment with such a Gothic view of nature is clear not only in their bacterial cause but also in their Morlock-esque affinity with many of those animal species that incite 'biophobia'[173] – most notably their affinity with bats and insects such as mosquitos. Neville de-*monstrates* the biological mechanisms of the vampire plague just as Horkheimer and Adorno's enlightenment scientist disenchants nature, and with much the same results. For while he succeeds in explaining the precise nature of the *vampiris* bacteria, Neville is nonetheless unable to foresee the new vampire society's violent takeover and his own entanglement with mythology as he becomes the terror-inducing 'legend' for these 'new people of the earth'.[174] The third term that arises from such a short-circuit dialectic is not, therefore, a posthuman one in the emancipatory sense often given to the term, exemplified by Haraway's notion of the cyborg as a site of 'transgressed boundaries, potent fusions, and dangerous possibilities'.[175] Rather, the new vampire society is the dialectic *becoming-that-which-it-already-is* of the enlightenment project, falling back upon both Neville *qua* humanity and the undead vampire *qua* nature to inflict its violence indiscriminately.

---

[171] Horkheimer and Adorno, *Dialectic*, pp. 6, 1, 2.
[172] Matheson, *I Am Legend*, pp. 29, 135, 61, 147.   [173] Small, 'Part 1', p. 233.
[174] Matheson, *I Am Legend*, p. 170.
[175] Donna J. Haraway, *Simians, Cyborgs, and Women: The Reinvention of Nature* (New York: Routledge, 1991), p. 154.

If there is a moment in which Neville demonstrates a sympathy that is at once posthuman and Gothic, it is not that with the dog or with the living vampires. Rather, Neville feels his most ontologically destabilising Other-oriented emotion in his sympathetic response to the undead vampires' suffering at the hands of the living vampires. In the penultimate scene of the novel, a team of living vampires assaults Neville's home, but before storming the barricaded dwelling they first gun down the undead vampires congregating in front. Watching through a peephole, Neville finds himself instinctively sympathising with the undead. His 'chest shudders with labored breath' as he watches the slaughter; his 'face twitche[s]' at the sound of the undead's screams. Where before Neville could not feel any sympathetic connection with these beings, as he regarded their atomistic movements as evidence of their aberrant and unsympathisable monstros-ity, Neville now feels both an instinctive empathic response and a compassionate disposition toward these creatures. He responds empathically to the sight of bullets taking down the undead, 'almost fe[eling] the bullets in his own flesh' and his 'body jerk[ing] with convulsive shudders', while he also comes to the conscious and compassionate 'realiz[ation] that he felt more deeply toward the [undead] vampires than he did toward their executioners'.[176] Here, Neville demonstrates that sympathetic impulse that undergirds the question that flows from Jeremey Bentham through Jacques Derrida to Donna Harraway – Can animals suffer?[177] By implicitly asking the Gothic version of such a question – Can the undead suffer? – Neville expands Bentham's circle of concern to the farthest reaches of the natural world. If the undead can suffer, can insects? Can plants? Coral? Bacteria and viruses? The non-living as well as the living? Such would be a form of sympathy truly akin to the 'monster' in Cohen's use of the term, for it too 'threatens to smash distinctions' between formerly distinct and disparate categories.

4.3 Conclusion: 'The Hero's the Bad One'

For Mathias Clasen, *I Am Legend*'s 'strong internal focalization with the protagonist … and its use of free indirect discourse as a window into his thoughts, emotions and inner struggles, all work toward facilitating empathy with Neville'.[178] This being true, then the reader should empathically share at least in part in both Neville's dialectic transformation and Neville's posthuman sympathies. Identifying with Neville *qua* representative for the human species, the reader should share in his experience of *becoming*-monster, should

---

[176] Matheson, *I Am Legend*, pp. 158–159.

[177] See Donna J. Haraway, *When Species Meet* (Minneapolis: University of Minnesota Press, 2008), pp. 19–27.

[178] Mathias Clasen, 'Vampire Apocalypse: A Biocultural Critique of Richard Matheson's *I Am Legend*', *Philosophy and Literature* 34:2 (October 2010): 313–328 (p. 317).

feel the weight of his monstrification on their own conscience. At the same time, the reader should sympathise with Neville's own sympathetic reactions to the suffering of others, should feel something in their own throat break at the death of the dog and feel their own body jerk with the suffering spasms of the undead. To confirm that readers generally share in this experience would of course require a lengthy reader response study, something far beyond the scope of this *Element*. Yet something like such a study in fact took place a half century after the novel's publication, and the results do not bode well for any hope in a widespread capacity for posthuman sympathy.

The events to which I refer were the test screenings of the 2007 film interpretation of *I Am Legend*, directed by Francis Lawrence and starring Will Smith as Robert Neville. The film differs in many ways from Matheson's original, but the central Gothic twist that sees Neville recognise his own monstrous villainousness is retained, at least in the version that was shown to the two original test audiences. The ending goes something like this: having chased them down into Neville's underground laboratory, the infected zombie-esque 'Darkseekers' have Neville and two other uninfected survivors trapped with no means of escape. All that stands between the Darkseekers and their apparent prey is a plexiglass wall, increasingly cracked and fragile with every blow from the alpha male of the Darkseeker pack. On the humans' side of the glass also lies a comatose Darkseeker woman, the most recent specimen to undergo Neville's consistently fatal experiments to find a cure. Just as all seems lost, the lead Darkseeker ceases to pound at the glass and instead smudges onto it an image of a butterfly. Neville stands puzzled for a moment before looking down to see a butterfly tattoo on the Darkseeker woman. Finally understanding, Neville wheels the infected woman out amongst the other members of the pack and proceeds to revive her, as all the while the Darkseekers growl and champ but refrain from harming him. Now awake, the Darkseeker woman shares a moment of distinctly animalistic affection with the alpha male, the two pressing their foreheads together and emitting strange mewling noises. The scene ends with the Darkseekers leaving with their liberated kin, but not before the alpha Darkseeker has barked his scornful condemnation at Neville. As the scientist recoils in shame down in the bottom right corner, the rest of the frame is dominated by a view of the far wall on which are hung a large collection of polaroids depicting Neville's previous Darkseeker victims.[179] As with the Neville of the novel, the Neville of the film undergoes a process of recognition of the Other that is at the same time a monstrification of the Self. Put simply,

---

[179] At time of writing, the original ending of the film can be watched on YouTube at the following link: www.youtube.com/watch?v=kPSk30qzgFs [last accessed 1 September 2023].

Neville experiences Gothic sympathy, and by sympathetic extension, so does the audience. How then did test audiences react to such a monstrifying sympathetic appeal?

Poorly, it seems. So poorly, in fact, that the ending was completely reshot and redone so that the theatrical release would end on a more traditionally heroic ending, in which the Darkseekers are not redeemed and Neville sacrifices himself to ensure the cure for the virus can reach a colony of human survivors. A decade after the film's release, Lawrence would reflect on the original ending of the film and the test audiences' reactions to it:

> I agree it's the better ending. I mean, it's the more philosophical version of the end, but in terms of story math we're doing everything you're not supposed to do, right? The hero doesn't find the cure, right? They drive off into the unknown and the creatures you've been saying are the bad ones the whole time you learn actually have humanity and aren't the bad ones – the hero's the bad one. And so you've basically turned everything on its head. We tested it twice and it got wildly rejected, wildly rejected, which is why we came out with the other one.[180]

For the test audiences, it seems, the Gothic sympathy of the twist ending was too uncomfortable to accept, whether because they could not bring themselves to sympathise with the Darkseekers or because they had invested too much of their sympathies into Will Smith's Neville to accept his sudden transformation into the monster. Like Wells's Time Traveller, the members of the test audience could not help but sympathise with the one who appeared most human and against those who seemed most inhuman, no matter how much their respective actions may have belied these appearances.

I close with this short discussion of the 2007 *I Am Legend* test screenings to underscore the contemporary relevance of the line of inquiry begun in this *Element*. In a world increasingly facing the consequences of climate change and other deleterious anthropocentric interventions into the natural world, the work of increasing our capacity to sympathise with those who will feel and are already feeling such consequences – human and non-human, animal and monster alike – takes on a moral urgency. And yet, we have seen that sympathy is as volatile as it is consoling, as fickle as it is powerful, as monstrous as it is humanising, and thus it is impractical to expect sympathy alone to serve as the panacea for all our ecological and social woes. The test screenings of *I Am Legend* serve as sobering warnings for any who might trust in the power of film, literature and other media to effect a wholesale transformation in human

---

[180] Quoted in Padraig Cotter, 'I Am Legend Director Reveals the Movie He Wishes He'd Made', Screenrant (22 January 2018). https://screenrant.com/i-am-legend-ending-approach/ [last accessed 1 September 2023].

consciousness and in our relations with each other and the natural world. Such media can act as potent and powerful tools, to be sure, and much can be gained from appealing to the sympathies of an audience; nonetheless, there are limits to such appeals, to which the *I Am Legend* test screening attest. These sympathetic limits have real-world consequences when we consider ecological conservation initiatives, for the test audiences' reactions to the sympathetic appeals of *I Am Legend* affirm Ernest Small's assertion that '[i]n the search for public support for conservation it is best not to bring up the negative images of hostile species' for though '[m]any species that seem very harmful to humans likely play useful roles in nature . . . it is probably futile to ask humans to sympathize with species that are very harmful to people'.[181] And yet, surely those harmful species must deserve our sympathy too? Are we capable, like the Robert Neville of Matheson's novel, to extend sympathy to creatures that are unwilling if not incapable of extending such sympathy back to us? Or will the looming threat of our own monstrification deter all but the bravest few in the audience from probing sympathy's Gothic depths? That such questions remain at the close of this study suggests that Gothic sympathy is a rich and timely site of inquiry, and while I hope to have shown that the Last Man texts discussed in this *Element* are a good starting place for such, they by no means exhaust the interpretive potential of this concept. Sympathy may be impossible to pin down or to rely on, but it is all the richer for this Gothic indeterminacy.

---

[181] Small, 'Part 2', pp. 51–52.

Bibliography

Airey, Jennifer L., *Religion Around Mary Shelley* (University Park: Pennsylvania University Press, 2019).

Alt, Christina, 'Extinction, Extermination, and the Ecological Optimism of H. G. Wells', in Gerry Canavan and Kim Stanley Robinson (eds.), *Green Planets: Ecology and Science Fiction* (Middletown: Wesleyan University Press, 2014), pp. 25–39.

Arnould-Bloomfield, Elisabeth, 'Posthuman Compassions', *PMLA* 130:5 (2015): 1467–1475.

Barton, Roman Alexander, Alexander Klaudies and Thomas Micklich, 'Introduction', in Roman Alexander Barton, Alexander Klaudies and Thomas Micklich (eds.), *Sympathy in Transformation: Dynamics Between Rhetorics, Poetics and Ethics* (Berlin, Boston: De Gruyter, 2018), pp. 1–16.

Batson, C. Daniel, 'These Things Called Empathy: Eight Related but Distinct Phenomena', in Jean Decety and William Ickes (eds.), *The Social Neuroscience of Empathy* (Cambridge, MA: MIT Press, 2009), pp. 3–15.

Bishop, Andrew, 'Making Sympathy "Vicious" on *The Island of Dr. Moreau*', *Nineteenth-Century Contexts* 43:2 (2021): 205–220.

Boddice, Rob, *The Science of Sympathy: Morality, Evolution, and Victorian Civilization* (Illinois: University of Illinois, 2016).

Britton, Jeanne M., *Vicarious Narratives: A Literary History of Sympathy, 1750–1850* (Oxford: Oxford University Press, 2019).

Bryn Jones Square, Shoshannah, 'The "victim of too much loving": Perdita Verney's Self-Destructive Sympathy in Mary Shelley's *The Last Man*', *Studies in Literary Imagination* 51:1 (Spring 2018): 61–78.

Burke, Edmund, *A Philosophical Enquiry Into the Origin of Our Ideas of the Sublime and Beautiful*, edited by Adam Phillips (Oxford: Oxford University Press, 1998).

Caldwell, Janis McLarren, *Literature and Medicine in Nineteenth-Century Britain: From Mary Shelley to George Eliot* (Cambridge: Cambridge University Press, 2004).

Cameron, Lauren, 'Mary Shelley's Malthusian Objections in *The Last Man*', *Nineteenth-Century Literature* 67:2 (September 2012): 177–203.

Cameron, Lauren, 'Questioning Agency: Dehumanizing Sustainability in Mary Shelley's *The Last Man*', in Ben P. Robertson (ed.), *Romantic Sustainability: Endurance and the Natural World, 1780–1830* (Maryland: Lexington Books, 2016), pp. 261–273.

Cantor, Paul A., 'The Apocalypse of Empire: Mary Shelley's *The Last Man*', in Sydney M. Conger, Frederick S. Frank and Gregory O'Dea (eds.), *Iconoclastic Departures: Mary Shelley After Frankenstein: Essays in Honor of the Bicentenary of Mary Shelley's Birth* (Madison: Fairleigh Dickinson University Press, 1997) pp. 193–211.

Clasen, Mathias, 'Vampire Apocalypse: A Biocultural Critique of Richard Matheson's *I Am Legend*', *Philosophy and Literature* 34:2 (October 2010): 313–328.

Cohen, Jeffrey Jerome, 'Monster Culture (Seven Theses)', in Asa Simon Mittman and Marcus Hensel (eds.), *Classic Readings on Monster Theory* (Leeds: Arc Humanities Press, 2020), pp. 43–54.

Cohen, Simchi, 'The Legend of Disorder: The Living Dead, Disorder and Autoimmunity in Richard Matheson's *I Am Legend*', *Horror Studies* 5:1 (2014): 47–63.

Cotter, Padraig, 'I Am Legend Director Reveals the Movie He Wishes He'd Made', *Screenrant* (22 January 2018). https://screenrant.com/i-am-legend-ending-approach/ [last accessed 1 September 2023].

Daffron, Benjamin Eric, *Romantic Doubles: Sex and Sympathy in British Gothic Literature 1790–1830* (New York: AMS Press, 2002).

de Staël, Germaine, *De L'Allemagne*, 3 vols (Paris: 1813), vol. 1. www.guten berg.org/cache/epub/66924/pg66924-images.html [last Accessed 16 August 2023].

Decety, Jean and William Ickes (eds.), *The Social Neuroscience of Empathy* (Cambridge, MA: MIT Press, 2009).

Deckard, Sharae, 'Ecogothic', in Maisha Webster and Xavier Aldana Reyes (eds.), *Twenty-First Century Gothic: An Edinburgh Companion* (Edinburgh: Edinburgh University Press, 2021), pp. 174–188.

Deren, Jennifer, 'Revolting Sympathies in Mary Shelley's *The Last Man*', *Nineteenth Century Literature* 72:2 (2017): 135–160.

Edward, Laura Hyatt, 'A Brief Conceptual History of Einfühlung: 18th-Century Germany to Post-World War II U.S. Psychology', *History of Psychology* 16:4 (2013): 269–281.

Faubert, Michelle, 'Challenging Sympathy in Mary Shelley's Fiction: *Frankenstein, Matilda*, and "The Mourner"', *English: Journal of the English Association* 71:275 (2022): 315–332.

Faubert, Michelle, 'The Fictional Suicides of Mary Wollstonecraft', *Literature Compass* 12:12 (2015): 652–659.

Faubert, Michelle, '*Werther* Goes Viral: Suicidal Contagion, Anti-Vaccination, and Infectious Sympathy', *Literature and Medicine* 34:2 (Fall 2016): 389–417.

Foley, Matt, *Gothic Voices: The Vococentric Soundworld of Gothic Writing* (Cambridge: Cambridge University Press, 2023).

Glasgow, Adryan, '"Wild Work": The Monstrosity of Whiteness in *I Am Legend*', in Cheyenne Mathews and Janet V. Haedicke (eds.), *Reading Richard Matheson: A Critical Survey* (Lanham, MD: Rowman & Littlefield, 2014), pp. 31–43.

Greenslade, William, *Degeneration, Culture and the Novel 1880–1940* (Cambridge: Cambridge University Press, 1994).

Godwin, William, *An Enquiry Concerning Political Justice*, edited by Mark Philp (Oxford: Oxford University Press, 2013).

Godwin, William, *Posthumous Works of the Author of a Vindication of the Rights of Woman*, 4 Vols (London: 1798), vol. 3. www.gutenberg.org/cache/epub/23233/pg23233-images.html [last accessed 16 August 2023].

Goss, Erin M., 'The Smiles that One Is Owed: Justice, Justine, and Sympathy for a Wretch', in Orrin N. C. Wang (ed.), *Frankenstein in Theory* (New York: Bloomsbury Academic, 2021), pp. 185–198.

Haraway, Donna J., *Simians, Cyborgs, and Women: The Reinvention of Nature* (New York: Routledge, 1991).

Haraway, Donna J., *When Species Meet* (Minneapolis: University of Minnesota Press, 2008).

Haslanger, Andrea, 'The Last Animal: Cosmopolitanism in *The Last Man*', *European Romantic Review* 27:5 (2016): 659–678.

Heise-von der Lippe, Anya, 'Introduction: Post/human/Gothic', in Anya Heise-von der Lippe (ed.), *Posthuman Gothic* (Cardiff: University of Wales Press, 2017), pp. 1–16.

Heise-von der Lippe, Anya, 'Posthuman Gothic', in Maisha Webster and Xavier Aldana Reyes (eds.), *Twenty-First Century Gothic: An Edinburgh Companion* (Edinburgh: Edinburgh University Press, 2021), pp. 218–230.

Horkheimer, Max and Theodor W. Adorno, *The Dialectic of Enlightenment*, trans. Edmund Jephcott, edited by Gunzelin Schmid Noeri (Stanford: Stanford University Press, 2002).

Hume, David, *A Treatise of Human Nature*. https://davidhume.org/texts/t/full [last accessed 1 September 2023].

Hume, Kathryn, 'Eat or be Eaten: H. G. Wells's *Time Machine*', *Philological Quarterly* 69:2 (Spring 1990): pp. 233–251.

Huntington, John, *The Logic of Fantasy: H. G. Wells and Science Fiction* (New York: Columbia University Press, 1982).

Hurley, Kelly, *The Gothic Body: Sexuality, Materialism, and Degeneration at the Fin de Siècle* (Cambridge: Cambridge University Press, 2004).

Keen, Suzanne, *Empathy and the Novel* (New York: Oxford University Press, 2007).

Knight, Rhonda, 'Evolving the Human in Richard Matheson's *I Am Legend* and M. R. Carey's Hungry Plague Novels', *Supernatural Studies: An Interdisciplinary Journal of Art, Media, and Culture* 7:1 (2021): 50–72.

Koenig-Woodyard, Chris, '"Lovie – is the vampire so bad?": Posthuman Rhetoric in Richard Matheson's *I Am Legend*', in Anya Heise-von der Lippe (ed.), *Posthuman Gothic* (Cardiff: University of Wales Press, 2017), pp. 77–92.

Koenig-Woodyard, Chris, 'The Mathematics of Monstrosity: Vampire Demography in Richard Matheson's *I Am Legend*, *University of Toronto Quarterly* 87:1 (Winter 2018): 81–109.

Kristeva, Julia, *Powers of Horror: An Essay on Abjection* (New York: Columbia University Press, 1982).

Lamb, Jonathan, *The Evolution of Sympathy in the Long Eighteenth Century* (London: Pickering & Chatto, 2009).

Lee, Michael Parish, 'Reading Meat in H. G. Wells', *Studies in the Novel* 42:3 (Fall 2010): 249–268.

Matheson, Richard, *I Am Legend* (New York: Tom Doherty Associates, 1995).

Marshall, David, *The Surprising Effects of Sympathy: Marivaux, Diderot, Rousseau, and Mary Shelley* (Chicago: The University of Chicago Press, 1988).

McLean, Steven, *The Early Fiction of H. G. Wells: Fantasies of Science* (New York: Palgrave Macmillan, 2009).

McWhir, Anne, 'Mary Shelley's Anti-Contagionism: *The Last Man* as "Fatal Narrative"', *Mosaic: An Interdisciplinary Critical Journal* 35:2 (June 2002): 23–38.

McWhir, Anne, 'Introduction', in Anne McWhir (ed.), *Mary Shelley: The Last Man* (Peterborough: Broadview, 1996), xiii–xxxvi.

Melville, Peter, 'The Problem of Immunity in "The Last Man"', *SEL: Studies in English Literature, 1500–1900* 47:4 (Autumn 2007): 825–846.

Mestas, Menina, 'The "Werther Effect" of Goethe's *Werther*: Anecdotal Evidence in Historical News Reports', *Health Communication* (2023): 1–6.

Paley, Morton D., '*The Last Man*: Apocalypse Without Millennium', in Anne K. Mellor (ed.), *The Other Mary Shelley: Beyond Frankenstein* (Oxford: Oxford University Press, 1993), pp. 107–123.

Phillips, David P., 'The Influence of Suggestion on Suicide: Substantive and Theoretical Implications of the Werther Effect', *American Sociological Review* 39:3 (June 1974): 340–354.

Philmus, Robert M. and David Y. Hughes (eds.), *H. G. Wells: Early Writings in Science and Science Fiction* (California: University of California Press, 1975).

Pick, Daniel, *Faces of Degeneration: A European Disorder, c. 1848 – c. 1918* (Cambridge: Cambridge University Press, 1989).

Quinn, Emelia, *Reading Veganism: The Monstrous Vegan, 1818 to Present* (Oxford: Oxford University Press, 2021).

Richardson, Rebecca, 'The Environmental Uncanny: Imagining the Anthropocene in Mary Shelley's *The Last Man*', *ISLE: Interdisciplinary Studies in Literature and Environment* 26:4 (Autumn 2019): pp. 1062–1083.

Shelley, Mary, *Frankenstein; or, the Modern Prometheus*, edited by David Lorne Macdonald and Kathleen Scherf (Peterborough: Broadview, 2012).

Shelley, Mary, *The Last Man*, edited by Anne McWhir (Peterborough: Broadview, 1996).

Shelley, Mary, *The Journals of Mary Shelley, 1814–1844*, edited by Paula R. Feldman and Diana Scott-Kilvert, 2 Vols (Oxford: Oxford University Press, 1987). www.nlx.com/collections/110> [last accessed 16 August 2023].

Small, Ernest, 'The New Noah's Ark: Beautiful and Useful Species Only. Part 1. Biodiversity Conservation Issues and Priorities', *Biodiversity* 12:4 (2011): 232–247.

Small, Ernest, 'The New Noah's Ark: Beautiful and Useful Species Only. Part 2. The Chosen Species', *Biodiversity* 13:1 (2012): 37–53.

Smith, Adam, *The Theory of Moral Sentiments*, edited by Knud Haakonssen (Cambridge: Cambridge University Press, 2002).

Smith, Andrew and William Hughes, 'Introduction: defining the ecoGothic', in Andrew Smith and William Hughes (eds.), *EcoGothic* (Manchester: Manchester University Press, 2013), pp. 1–14.

Snyder, Robert Lance, 'Apocalypse and Indeterminacy in Mary Shelley's "The Last Man"', *Studies in Romanticism* 17:4 (Fall 1978): 435–452.

Stephanou, Aspasia, '"The Last of the Old Race": *I Am Legend* and Bio-Vampire-Politics', in Cheyenne Mathews and Janet V. Haedicke (eds.), *Reading Richard Matheson: A Critical Survey* (Lanham, MD: Rowman & Littlefield, 2014), pp. 17–28.

Sterrenburg, Lee, '*The Last Man*: Anatomy of a Failed Revolution', *Nineteenth-Century Fiction* 33:3 (December 1978): 324–347.

Thorson, Jan and Per-Anne Öberg, 'Was there a Suicide Epidemic after Goethe's *Werther*?' *Archives of Suicide Research* 7:1 (2003): 69–72.

Valentine, Colton, 'H. G. Wells and the *Fin-de-Siècle* Gustatory Paradox', *The Review of English Studies* 71:302 (2020): 937–951.

Vargo, Lisa, 'Male and Female Werthers: Romanticism and Gothic Suicide', in William Hughes and Andrew Smith (eds.), *Suicide and the Gothic* (Manchester: Manchester University Press, 2019), pp. 36–51.

Vint, Sherryl, 'Animals and Animality from the Island of Moreau to the Uplift Universe', *The Yearbook of English Studies* 37:2 (2007): 85–102.

Wagar, W. Warren, *Terminal Visions: The Literature of Last Things* (Bloomington: Indiana University Press 1982).

Wagner-Lawlor, Jennifer A., 'Performing History, Performing Humanity in Mary Shelley's *The Last Man*', *SEL: Studies in English Literature 1500–1900* 42:4 (Autumn 2002): 753–780.

Wells, H. G., *Certain Personal Matters*. www.gutenberg.org/files/17508/17508-h/17508-h.htm> [last accessed 1 September 2023].

Wells, H. G., *The Island of Doctor Moreau*, edited by Mason Harris (Peterborough: Broadview Press, 2009).

Wells, H. G., *The Time Machine*, edited by Nicholas Ruddick (Peterborough: Broadview Press, 2001).

Wells, H. G., *The War of the Worlds*, edited by Martin A. Danahay (Peterborough: Broadview Press, 2003).

Cambridge Elements ☰

The Gothic

Dale Townshend
Manchester Metropolitan University
Dale Townshend is Professor of Gothic Literature in the Manchester Centre for Gothic Studies, Manchester Metropolitan University.

Angela Wright
University of Sheffield
Angela Wright is Professor of Romantic Literature in the School of English at the University of Sheffield and co-director of its Centre for the History of the Gothic.

Advisory Board

About the Series
Seeking to publish short, research-led yet accessible studies of the foundational 'elements' within Gothic Studies as well as showcasing new and emergent lines of scholarly enquiry, this innovative series brings to a range of specialist and non-specialist readers some of the most exciting developments in recent Gothic scholarship.

Cambridge Elements ≡

The Gothic

Elements in the Series

Gothic Voices
Matt Foley

Mary Robinson and the Gothic
Jerrold E. Hogle

Folk Gothic
Dawn Keetley

The Last Man and Gothic Sympathy
Michael Cameron

A full series listing is available at: www.cambridge.org/GOTH

Printed in the United States
by Baker & Taylor Publisher Services